An entertaining perspective delivered through clever storytelling delivers valuable insight into essential life lessons often overlooked in the busyness of today's world. A great refresher for anyone seeking financial independence and self-discipline, in conjunction with support from their own personal taxation and financial advisors. An essential read for school leavers and university graduates embarking on their working life.

-- Kylie Lamprecht, Pitcher Partners

Self-reliance in this rapidly changing world needs a plan. To generate that plan, you need to understand the environment in which you are living, understand who you are, attain the required skills and then create a vision for yourself.

The vision needs to balance lifestyle, job satisfaction, what you earn, how you are perceived by others and your own moral code. Getting the balance is what you learn at The Parallel University.

The Parallel University
Create a balanced life and have it all

Richard Krohn

Connor Court Publishing

Published in 2018 by Connor Court Publishing

Copyright © Richard Krohn

All rights reserved. No part of this book may be reproduced or transmitted in any form or by any means, electronic or mechanical, including photocopying, recording or by any information storage and retrieval system, without prior permission in writing from the publisher.

Connor Court Publishing Pty Ltd
PO Box 7257
Redland Bay QLD 4165
sales@connorcourt.com

www.connorcourtpublishing.com.au

Phone 0497 900 685

ISBN: 9781925826111

Cover design: Samy Therone

Printed in Australia

General Advice Warning
The information contained in this book is general in nature and does not consider your personal situation. You should consider whether the information is appropriate to your needs, and where appropriate, seek professional advice from a financial adviser or other professional advisor.
Taxation, legal and other matters referred to in this book are of a general nature only and are based on the author's interpretation of laws existing at the time and should not be relied upon in place of appropriate professional advice. Those laws may change from time to time. Some laws have changed since writing.

Accuracy & Reliability of Information
Although every effort has been made to verify the accuracy of the information contained in this book, the author disclaims all liability (except for any liability which by law cannot be excluded), for any error, inaccuracy in, or omission from the information contained in this book or any loss or damage suffered by any person directly or indirectly through relying on this information.

*To the next generation,
in the hope that they can create
the balanced life of their dreams*

About the Author

After completing a BSc, Richard Krohn started his career working in industry and government, trying to save the world from pollution. Richard quickly learned that regulation and legislation was never going to solve the problem.

More to the point an understanding that small contributions from many is far more powerful than massive contributions by a few. Richard wrote *The Parallel University* as an introduction to the new world for those beginning on the journey.

Contents

Preface		9
1	The New Game	13
2	Your Environment	19
3	Balance	101
4	Fifty things I have learned	105
5	Finance	133
6	Business basics	147
7	Investment basics	155
8	Who are you?	215
9	Your vision	227
10	Your Plan	231
11	A Standard Plan	241
Conclusion		255
Epilogue		257
A Schedule		259

Preface

This book was written for those between the ages of 18 and 30, because by the time you are 30 years of age you will have made one of the most important decisions of your life, probably without even knowing that you made it.

Mainstream education focuses on politics, culture, technology, finance, society and how you fit in. It focuses on what you can do to change the world. This book focuses on what you can do to plan your life to achieve your aims in terms of lifestyle, job satisfaction, finance, kudos and ethics.

We live in a world where 20% of people support the other 80%. Most us are supported by our parents while at school. Over 60% of families pay no net tax and 80% of retirees receive a full or part pension. Society started welfare to help those who cannot help themselves. What does it say about our society when 80% of it cannot look after itself?

In the world there are those that make it happen, those that watch it happen and those that wonder what did happen.

The Parallel University was written to give you the skills to start a social movement toward self-reliance and self fulfillment. We all want to feel useful, and our greatest use is to not be a burden on society. And that is only the starting point. We will see how the world is moving back to being controlled by capital and not by income, therefore to be able to not only be self-reliant but also be capable of ensuring your families are self-reliant you will need to build a capital base.

Make no mistake to be able to achieve that you will need to swim against the tide of modern politics, culture, and finance. Modern governments seem determined to discourage the accumulation of capital through saving. Modern culture seems to focus on what can be extracted from society rather than what you can add, and the global finance world has developed into a giant spinning wheel where the money at the edges flies off into the arms of the finance industry leaving the core depleted.

The load you will need to carry in order to look after yourself and your family will be heavy. You will be an outsider and you will be ridiculed by the majority. However, when you retire from day to day work and know that you will still remain a contributor to society instead of a burden you will feel useful, you will feel enriched and you will be able to carry your head high.

Imagine a federal budget that was stripped of the need to support 80% of society. Imagine those funds being channelled into better infrastructure, better education, and health.

You do not have to earn more, all you must do is to manage your resources in a more efficient and proactive manor.

Should you choose to become self-reliant and not spend your life leaning on society you will need to use what Einstein called the greatest power on earth. Compound interest will drive you towards your objectives given time. Leave the starting date too long and that power is stripped from you and you will end up like most retirees spending their capital on holidays and upgrading their houses so that they can get their assets and income under the caps for pension benefits.

Financial freedom starts with earning more than you spend and then investing it in the right structure and with a rate of return that meets your objectives. Running your own finances is simply not that hard, however the vast majority outsource this function to others at a huge cost. Fees of 1% over your lifetime equate to $1mill less in your retirement account. The average superannuant has paid advisors, and financial institutions between 3 and 4% over the last 30 years. That is the difference of retiring with $4mill or $350,000. The more tasks you undertake yourself the shorter the distribution chain and the lower the fees you pay. The fees you do pay need to go to a trusted and reliable service provider.

Be aware that during your life you will earn more from investment income than you will from wages. So why wouldn't you spend a little time each week on your major source of life long income. It doesn't need to be a passion, but it does need to be interesting. That interest comes from achieving objectives and creating the lifestyle of your dreams.

It was only 110 years ago that over 85% of the world's population lived in poverty. For hundreds of thousands of years mankind has focused on survival and in the space of 100 years the human environment has changed dramatically however our physiology and psychology hasn't kept in step.

You have a body and a mind that has been fined tuned for survival, yet you no longer need to use these skills. So, what are you going to use your inherent skills for?

Humans have a desire inbuilt into their DNA to be useful. If you cannot be useful surviving, then how are you going to be useful? Many people today think they are being useful by trying to change the society in which we live. With 7.5 billion people on the planet that is a huge task. We do have the ability to be useful by not leaning on others in society. The simple task of making your way through life without calling on others for help is a very useful objective.

For 600,000 years we have been programmed to survive. That programming still exists in our DNA. Let's redefine survival. Let's say survival is taking responsibility for yourself and looking after yourself and your family. If we all did that then society would change into a form that most of us crave. Therefore, it would be a great start if we thought of the definition of being useful as being self-reliant.

I would go one step further and say that the greatest moral challenge for your age is to take responsibility for yourself and ensure that you have a positive political, financial, cultural and physical effect on the society and environment in which you live. If at present only 20% of the population manage to achieve that goal imagine the positive effect on the world if we could increase that to 50% one by one starting with you.

1
The New Game

Just over 100 years ago 85% of the world lived in poverty and life expectancy for an Australian was around 55 years. There was no middle class, you either had capital or you didn't. The industrial revolution happened and the whole game changed from a game of capital to a game of income. WWII accelerated the game by growing the middle class. In the 60's and 70's and even into the 80's a house cost three to four times a single annual salary. Education expenses were minimal. Fuel, power, rates and insurance were dirt cheap compared to today. Most people worked until they were 60 to 65 and only had a few years retirement which was easily paid for out of their accumulated assets.

The game has now changed. Today 8.4% of the world's population live in poverty. The median house price is over 10 times the average salary. The cost of child care and education has skyrocketed. The regulatory demands of ESG (Environmental, Social, Governance.) and CSR (Corporate Social Responsibilities.) issues has increased the costs of power, rates, insurance and building by three to four times over the last decade. On top of that you are expected to live until you are 90 and therefore need to fund your retirement for about 20 years. Or you can rely on the aged pension which at present is about $30,000per annum for a couple.

Two major things have changed. The first is that the game has swung back from income to capital. The advent of AI (Artificial Intelligence) will dramatically curtail the salaries for the vast majority, and therefore it will become increasingly difficult for an individual to work their way to financial success. The other major change is that the three demands of housing, education and retirement all need the power of compound interest, doing one at a time is just not going to cut it in the future.

Hitting the trifecta of owning your own home, educating children and having a comfortable retirement has just got a lot more difficult and requires you to begin the process as early as possible.

Winston Churchill was quoted as saying that if you were not a socialist when you were 20 you had no heart, but if you remained a socialist when you were 40 you had no brain. Unfortunately, that is no longer relevant because if you wait until you are in your mid thirties to get with the program you have lost 15 valuable years that you just cannot get back.

Given the present political environment you do have a choice. You can run with the left and rely on government support, or you can stand up and take responsibility. And this is where your greatest dilemma comes in.

There are several basics of psychology that need to be understood:

1. Personal satisfaction only comes when you step outside your comfort zone.
2. Your brain constantly talks to you in negatives. Fulfillment only comes when you can deal with your own thoughts.
3. The human brain is hardwired to survive. Take away the drive to survive and you take away the meaning of life.

If you chose to rely on society then you take away the meaning of life. If you chose to take responsibility for yourself and your family, you will give yourself a life filled with hard work and oppression.

So, it's up to you to pick up the load and carry it or sit back and enjoy the ride at somebody else's expense.

How to Play the new game

The answer to that is simple:

As you would play any other game.

First you need to understand the rules.

Second, be aware of the environment, the playing conditions.

Third, become aware of yourself.

Fourth, develop a skill base.

Fifth, beg borrow or steal the equipment required.

Sixth, develop a game plan.

Seventh, implement the plan irrespective of what is happening on the field.

The Rules

For this game the rules are simple.

It is wired into your DNA to procreate and to survive. However, as a life form we have moved on a little from Neanderthal man and our sphere of influence has extended to family and the next generations.

The rules become simple:

1. Do what you can to look after yourself. (Carry the load.)
2. Do what you can to look after your family and its future generations. (Carry an even greater load.)
3. Play nice. (Used to be do unto others as you would have them do unto you.)
4. Reduce the suffering of others. (Pay it forward.)

What more do you need?

Your Environment

Your environment is the political, economic, cultural and physical environment in which you live.

In understanding the world, you also need to learn where we came from and the language that we use. You need to understand how the economy, the law and the culture of your environment works.

You wouldn't plan a short term holiday overseas without checking the climate, the currency, cultural requirements and the equipment you will need.

Skills

The skills are what you will need to make and implement the plan. Also, I have added some things that I have learned that may be of help along your journey.

When you learn a language, you start with the alphabet. When you learn math, you start with the times table. If you have the fundamental basics of the language at your fingertips, you can navigate through the subjects with ease.

Become Aware of Yourself

In your plan you are the creator, the administrator and the technician. More on that later.

You will have your own unique balance of your needs for job satisfaction, lifestyle, kudos, financial reward and ethics. The determination of who you are will lead to your strengths and weaknesses. These lead to your strategic competitive advantages.

Equipment

One of the basic rules of creating wealth is to get the structure correct. You need to imagine what your structure looks like after retirement, yes that is 50 years down the line. Getting the structure wrong early is the equivalent of learning to play golf with a hockey stick. You may get by in the short term but later it will have a distinctly negative effect.

The Plan

Planning needs a mission and a vision. The mission is a simple statement of what you are trying to achieve. In business the mission is a statement of what business you are in.

The vision must have a quantity and a timeframe.

Your mission and vision will be divided into the five sectors:
1. Job Satisfaction. Career.
2. Lifestyle.
3. Kudos.
4. Financial Rewards.
5. Ethics.

Reframing Your Values and Philosophies

Because of the advent of linguistic constructivism, we are never quite sure of where we are. Our thought patterns have been changed in everything we do, in everything we see and in everything that we hear. To define what you believe you need to be able to debate a point from both sides. Once you have developed solid arguments from opposite perspectives you have a chance of developing your personal position.

We need to understand what is real and what needs to be questioned.

None of these sections are meant to be an exhaustive analysis, they are simply there to set a scene and try to get you to question your environment, yourself and deliver a vision and plan for your future.

2

Your Environment

It's a brave new world. The problem is that we are having issues fathoming just how brave and how new.

To create a plan for your life you need to be aware of the world in which you live. You need to understand the boundaries, the systems and the physical environment in which you are living and in which you will live in the future.

The world is changing at an amazing rate, technology, population and education are bounding ahead. We need to have a rough idea of where we have come from and where we are going. You cannot devise a plan for your future if you do not understand the parameters of the world in which you are going to live that plan.

I have heard it said that memories/history are there to teach us lessons. No one person is smart enough to play the game from scratch and get it all correct. Nature and the world is far too complex for one brain. Therefore, we need to read and understand from those who have gone before in order to make the most of our situation.

Physical

The earth on which we live is 510m square kilometres, of which 71% is covered by water. Of the land component 33% is uninhabitable desert and 24% is too mountainous. This leaves 15.8 billion acres on which for us to live. There are 7.5 billion people living on earth, across 195 different countries, speaking up to 6,500 languages. Between 7.5 billion, we get roughly 8,000 square metres each. In that 8,000 square metres, we must live, grow food, work, as well as travel and recreate.

Government

The governing of many people has always been an issue. Over the last few millenniums any number of methods of governing have been tried. In the early days of civilisation areas, countries were normally ruled by strength as depicted on *Game of Thrones*. Over centuries authoritarian government was proven to be fruitful in times of troubles, given the right leader or leaders. However, in times of peace they were found to breed corruption, be inefficient and aggressive.

An authoritarian style of government caused any number of problems from the leader being killed to succession issues. After centuries of rule by monarchs, autocrats and soldiers, more modern societies moved to other forms of government.

The problem with the transition was that vast numbers of people were imprisoned, killed and tortured. There was nothing kind or peaceful about the French or Russian revolutions. We should also remember that in both these cases there was an uprising of the peasants against the wealthy rulers. Both revolutions had unintended consequences.

The French ended the revolution with Napoleonic rule, back to an autocrat. And the Russian revolution ended with a communist government. In both cases the peasants ended up worse off and without the democratic rule they hoped for.

It is important to realise that up until the industrial revolution at the end of the nineteenth century over 95% of the population lived in poverty and therefore they spent the vast majority of their time simply trying to feed themselves and their families. Therefore, most people had little if any interest in political issues especially international political issues.

Democracy has been famously quoted as a highly flawed system of governance but way in front of whatever runs second.

The Present

Individual nations have tried a number of different systems of government over the last 150 years. There are any number of issues that have been debated over the centuries from secular government to the separation of powers, voting characteristics, powers of the head of state versus the power of the legislator.

There is one constant and that is summed up in the quote by Ronald Reagan. "Freedom is never more than one generation away from extinction. We didn't pass it to our children in the bloodstream. It must be fought for, protected, and handed on to them to do the same." In other words we can spend generations fighting for something but it only takes one generation to end it.

This quote does not just apply to freedom it also applies to the separation of powers and secular government as ideas and ideals.

The end of the second world war in 1945 was the start of a march toward International government. While individual nations have their own systems of government an international system is being developed.

The world recognised that with the munitions that had been developed during the world wars it was unthinkable for another world war to eventuate. We simply had to have a system that could control potential worldwide conflicts. As a result, the UN was born.

Many saw globalism as a vehicle for driving equality. Funds need to be taken from the richer nations and given to the poor. There have been several distinct problems with this with the main one being the transactional costs. Unfortunately, the poorer nations seem to have more corrupt, inefficient and aggressive governments and therefore the distribution of wealth doesn't always go according to plan.

There is no doubt that globalism has failed. I do not think you will find anybody that thinks the UN is an efficient governing body. The problem is where to from here, and that seems to be divided into two camps.

The first camp is the progressives who believe we need to move forward. Their answer is to throw out the concept of nations and make the world one big family. The key driver to make this work will be the universal wage. They argue that AI (Artificial Intelligence) will result in about 80% of the workforce out of a job. The huge productivity increases that result from AI will allow for the total population of the world to receive a universal wage. That will be a government payment that will ensure we all start from an equal base. While the progressives have no answer to what all these people will do they see that the national system was a failure and that the logical way forward is an international governance system. The downside of that argument is written in the Tower of Babel, one of those stories in that book called The Bible people used to read. When you have a chain of command that reaches over many languages, many cultures and many levels of government it must fail.

The conservatives on the other hand believe that international governance has floundered and therefore it is better to take one step back after taking two steps forwards. They believe that we need to regroup, think about our native instincts and play to the strengths built into our DNA.

In summary today we have a world with 195 countries with almost as many types of government. These countries have been drawn together in international bodies that have failed to find an efficient form of global government.

Politics

I read somewhere that politics is always fought on the biggest issue of the day. There are in fact to my pragmatic mind three major issues driving world politics of the early 21st Century.

Equality

Humans are not equal. We all know that from the first days in the school yard. I know some people talk about equality as being equality of opportunity, well that is as daft as equality of people. Some people see an opportunity around every corner and others would not see it if it ran over them. You have to actually see the opportunity before you can use it.

If you think there is a glass ceiling in your room, maybe you are in the wrong room.

Globalism

Will government in the near future move further towards globalism or retreat to nationalism? Globalism has not lead to level playing fields. From the very beginning of free trade pacts there have been winners and losers. Globalism and economic rationalism have taken away the reason for living in the hearts and minds of many. The meaning of life for many is the ability to survive and support yourself and your family. Free trade pacts have taken that reason for their being away from many in the developed world and transferred it to many more in the undeveloped world. If you think that can happen without some sort of rear guard action you will be mistaken.

The left wing has always been hell bent on readjusting the sharing of the pie. The right wing has focused on increasing the size of the pie. The heart of wealth redistribution has been the taking from some to give to others. Any sustainable system of government needs to increase the size of the pie so as it can share the love around without the result being detrimental to any group, especially those generating the wealth.

Identity Politics

The problem is that identity politics identifies people by the colour of their skin, their sexual orientation, their social background or any other number of factors. Liberal thinkers have fought for centuries so that each and every person can be identified as themselves not as part of a group.

The focus on identity politics has moved the discussion back ten paces.

Some people want to be defined by a group. They believe we all should be equal and that nobody should stand out of the crowd. These are the people that perpetually feel oppressed, they feel society should look after them and they want the safety of numbers. To these people a universal wage would be a god send. They wouldn't have to compete.

Most people want to define themselves. They are happy to occasionally become part of a group to carry out a skill or activity, but they do not want to be defined by the group.

Australian government

Australia is a federal parliamentary constitutional monarchy. The country is divided into 150 areas, supposedly of roughly the same number of people, called electorates. Each electorate gets to vote in one member to the House of Representatives. The country is also divided into states and territories. Each state gets to vote in 12 senators and each territory 2 senators. It is the job of the House of Representatives to enact legislation that runs the country. It used to be the job of the senate to review that legislation to make sure that it does not have unintended consequences or is a howler.

In other words, the House of Representatives is the field umpire and the senate is the third umpire up in the stands. However, of recent times the third umpire has started to make its own decisions independently of the field umpire.

The cost of government in Australia has gotten well out of control. In a world that is working towards an international government to govern over 8 billion people in Australia we have three levels of government for 24 million people. There are three major issues that need to be addressed.

Debate

The art of debate has been deliberately stricken from the political agenda. There are a couple of reasons for this apart from the obvious that when a party feels they cannot win a debate they change the rules.

Facts

Once upon a time a fact was a fact, but no more. Facts can be changed in several ways:

Social constructivism versus logic

Those that practice Identity Politics are good at constructing a narrative that suites their argument. A constructed argument cannot be questioned because it is, that is it exists and therefore cannot be questioned.

Social Constructivism is an educational theory of acquiring knowledge which emphasises the importance of culture and context in and constructing knowledge. Jean Piaget's constructivist theory stated that humans cannot be given information which they immediately understand and use. Instead, humans must construct their own knowledge. They build their knowledge through experience. This led to Richard Rorty writing "objectivity is a matter of intersubjective consensus among human beings, not of accurate representation of something non-human."

It appears that many academics throughout the world have latched onto Piaget's theory and wound it up about ten notches until it comes out basically saying that truth was a function of human consensus and could not be measured by scientific measurements.

Unfortunately, it has become a fact that intent science has taken over from logical science, where reasoning conducted or assessed according to strict principles of validity. Where validity refers to how well a scientific test or piece of research actually measures what it sets out to, or how well it reflects the reality it claims to represent.

From a purely political point of view we have some politicians working on facts that have been created through the process of constructivism, while others argue from a pure logical base. Therefore, there can be no discussion and no debate because the premise of one side is discounted by the other. We might as well be talking in two different languages.

This point cannot be stressed enough. We see it in politics all around the world.

It is become incredibly clear in Australia with the debate on free speech. The language of the right is that I may not like what you have to say but I will defend your right to say it. The language of the left says that if we discuss something that may cause offense to anybody then it should not be discussed. There is logic in both languages, however if we take the view of the right to the absurd then anybody can say anything to anyone and that is culturally unacceptable. And if we take the left to an extreme we forfeit all ability to debate anything. These discussions used to be defined by the rules of religion, which grew into cultural traditions, however now that our society has discarded the ten commandments it requires our system of governance to define the ability to debate.

Statistics

We all know there are lies damn lies and statistics. You can do just about anything you like with a set of numbers. Whether it is the temperature of the earth, the income of the average person or the percentage of the population that pays tax. The aim today is never to compare one set of figures with another.

Language

When we travel to the US or UK we think that the language is the same, but it isn't. The same is true within Australia. Different people use the same words for different reasons. These variations can occur over professions, geographic areas of cultural beliefs.

We look at equality briefly below. The same word can mean a number of things to a number of people.

Equality

Our education system seems to have instilled an unnatural desire for equality. What is equality anyway. Line up 20 kids in a row and get them to sprint 100 metres. There will be a natural variation in times. Equality means telling the fastest that they must slow down so the whole group can finish together.

I'll tell you what equality meant two generations ago. I found myself in a small town in Yorkshire in 1977. I was visiting the town because I was visiting a prospective employer who had a job for me in Uganda. We went to the local pub on the Saturday night and I found myself listening to a guy about my age who was crying in his beer. Asked what the problem was he said that K Mart had just opened in Leeds, the nearest city. He went on to explain he was the local carpenter/joiner and everybody was going to Leeds to buy furniture instead of getting him to make it. So being a naïve Australian I asked why he didn't do something else. He explained he was the local joiner, his father had been the local joiner, his grandfather had been the local joiner and therefore the town dictated that he would be the local joiner. He couldn't take any other job because that would put someone else out of a job. He then explained there were only two ways out, gaol or the military. That was that sort of inequality that liberals fought against in the twentieth century, not the contrived equality that is put forward today.

The simple answer is that government can give everybody an education, they can give everybody a chance but to think for one minute that you can make everybody equal is simply absurd.

Where is politics going?

After reading and listening over the last few years it is clear that in general terms politics is moving to the left. That is a function of the growth of the middle class. We no longer need to work ten hours a day to feed ourselves. Productivity has increased and therefore food abounds as does power, transport and recreation. Life is good and therefore people feel it is possible to share the wealth around. When there is "spare" money we are happy to give it away to those that are perceived to be in need. So, when once the political spectrum thought in terms of left and right, they now think more in terms of theory versus practice. The left used to think only that we should all be equal and that in concert with the socialist belief that the government should control capital and production made for a great argument for the workers to take over capital from the business owners and control the economy. At the same time the right believed that by nature we are different and therefore we should have a system where capitalists use capital in the most efficient way and that will create enough for all through free market forces.

So we had the working class on one side and the conservative right capitalists on the other. In the 50's and 60's the middle class was driven by income. Those that saved part of their income had money and those that spent it were the have-nots.

Then the economy grew and there was more of it, whatever it may be. At the same time, more and more people went to university. The major explosion was in the humanities side of the spectrum. There were graduates in economics, politics and philosophy coming out of the university system at a huge rate. Now some of these were from families on the right and some from families on the left.

Therefore, especially in the 70s and 80s, we had thousands of Uni graduates pouring out into the world. Now for the humanitarians there were few if any jobs in the real world and therefore most of these went to work for either the government or non-government charities. And hence there was a huge cohort of educated "professionals" foisted upon the community all with left leaning tendencies, that ended up as teachers or public servants. These became the elites who, in their minds, were born to rule because they had a greater grip on the issues of the day than the uneducated workers and capitalists.

Some of these elites came from the socialist left and some came from the capitalist right. They all thought that the status quo was all wrong and therefore thought we needed to change and we needed to change fast. As a result, we ended up with a political class that were intellectuals and progressive.

The working class did not go to university they became tradesmen and ended up earning far more than the unemployable elites. They had a left-wing background but suddenly had wealth. This group had aspirations. They wanted to bring up their families with wealth. They wanted to travel, to educate their children and to save for their retirement. This was a new middle class that came from the working class and financially were leapfrogging over the progressive intellectuals. This became the pragmatic class, while their roots were in the left they realised that the only way to get ahead was to work and save. They still consider the Labor Party their home even though they cannot identify the theoretical considerations that the Labor politicians expound. They remain conservative, they remain left wing, but their minds have taken over from their hearts and they have dropped their socialist views.

The old right wingers went on to invest capital and create businesses. These are the capitalists that even though many have philanthropic objectives ultimately believe that it is only through individual endeavour that wealth can be created. These remain conservative, capitalist and right-wing. They are the delcons.

Some of the working class that did go to university made it in the commercial world and built a capital base.

In the middle of this, globalisation came along, and in

countries like Australia many of the working-class jobs were exported. Manufacturing industry moved out of Australia and with it literally millions of jobs. The elites thought this was great, Australians should not have to do these mundane jobs, but there was nothing there to replace them so the people that did not have the training for "the new jobs" had nowhere to go and they felt lost and useless.

Make no mistake politics has taken two decisive and aggressive turns. If you take the left globalism view we are headed for a future where the world government will be run by unelected elites and the majority of people will survive on a Universal wage with no real meaning in life. The right believe that we need to regroup as self motivated individuals who choose to carry their own loads, bonded into democratic nations who negotiate with each other.

The future is in your hands so you had better understand both sides and make an objective decision based on real facts and not a subjective decision based on linguistic constructivism.

The skills required for governing

In government you need firstly the dreamer, the person with the vision and ideas for the future. This person must embrace risk and reach for the stars. Then there is the administrator. The person to make sure that the pennies are counted and that the processes and procedures are adhered to. And then there is the technician. This is the person that actually knows how to do the job.

The visionary

In this fast-changing world, it is becoming more difficult to be a true visionary. Where will you be technically in 20 years' time, the mind boggles. In a political sense, we also need to know where present politics is driving society and how we are going to pull up out of the dive. Politics has descended into a bunch of slogans over the last decade. We are heading into a period where the government needs to explain our environment and what is needed for us to achieve our dreams. That means we need someone who can see where we are going and then put in place policies that will get us to that place. Someone with blinding persistence and courage. The Bible is a book of stories, Moses leading the Israelites into the promised land comes to mind.

The Administrator

Government needs to be efficient, frugal and well organised. The brain required for that is vastly different to the brain of the leader or entrepreneur. The administrator must be steeped in process.

The Technician

Somebody has to actually know how to do the job, to implement the policies. In the past, successful businesspeople who knew how to do things went to parliament to help get things done. Successful engineers, farmers, miners, builders and manufacturers went into politics not to be leaders but to give of their knowledge.

The Jobs of Government

Policy

The first stage of governing is creating policies. The government has to have a vision for the country, and it has to convert that vision into policies that will lead the country to achieve the objectives. This requires a dreamer.

Actions

The actual administration of the policies requires someone that can do the job, and has the know-how and the experience.

Affairs of state

Requires a cool mind that can negotiate and come up with new solutions based on the future goals of the parties involved.

Interaction of governing and law

Australia was brought into federation by a group of 13 men. The leader, Henry Parkes, was a labourer and a poet before joining politics. The other twelve comprised of three businessmen, a doctor, four farmers, one of whom was a cleric, and another a military captain trained at Sandhurst, a merchant mariner and three lawyers, one of whom was also an engineer. This is in stark contrast to the cabinet of today, where there are 12 lawyers, six political staffers, a public servant, an accountant, a policeman and a fisherman.

The shadow cabinet features 11 lawyers, with seven political staffers, three public servants and a unionist.

We know that law is based on precedent and apportionment of blame, and governing is based on creating a vision and defining policies to achieve that vision. Can no one see the blinding gap between the skills needed for government and the skills in our government?

What is the result of changing our politicians from business people to lawyers when, well, let's look no further than the big issue of the day and that is energy.

The prime minister wants to drag out an old plan for the snowy scheme that will produce about the same amount of power that was taken off line with the closing of Hazelwood. That means he wants to revisit the past to produce enough power to maintain the status quo. There is nothing about the future nothing about growth. We have 200,000 immigrants coming into the country each year and we already are short of power. No new ideas, no vision no direction just a blast from the past that had been written off as uneconomical.

But wait there is more: the Opposition leader wants to double the renewables that cost three times as much as the present power and he wants to pay for it by, wait for it, an emissions trading scheme. Now we are not going into emissions trading schemes (ETSs) and carbon taxes here but you do the research and you will see they are an apportionment of blame. The Opposition lawyers have ruled that emitting carbon is an offense, based on precedent, and that the offenders must pay in proportion with the amount that they offend. There is no thought of who ultimately pays. There is no thought to the future sources of efficient power and no thought to the allowing the free market to rule. Now most people reading this have not been brought up in a free market world so let's just describe that world for a minute. In a free market, you would have a number of electricity suppliers who would supply power to the grid at their cost of production plus a margin. Then you would have consumers who would buy that electricity according to their values and beliefs. Someone who is passionate about carbon dioxide would choose to pay three times as much for their power because of the good it would do to the environment. Somebody else may choose to buy the cheapest power available. Because we live in a socialist world where we are told by the government what we should think, we naturally all believe in the voice of the loudest and want to pay more for our power.

A number of years ago in Switzerland, we were in a store looking for honey. There were two products one was twice the price of the other. I asked what they sold and was told that nine out of ten sales were for the expensive locally produced product. That is a free market.

If you go through the issues of the day, any day, you will see the politics is dragged down by precedent and apportionment of blame. The focus on how to work together, how to synergise and build a better and greater country has gone.

Governance versus Politics

Recapping, governance is the action or manner of conducting the policy, actions and affairs of a state with authority. These are the processes of governing, while Politics is the activities aimed at improving someone's status or power within the government.

The job politicians are elected to do is to govern. Parents govern at home they draw up the plans of what the family is going to do and then they follow through on those plans. So you, as the constituent, tell your parents you want to go to an Adele concert. The government agrees and then draws up the rules of how that is going to happen, who you can go with, how you are going to get there and who pays.

However, before the parents agree your younger sibling says they want to go to. Mum says no. The sibling then comes to you and asks whether you mind if they go as well, you reluctantly agree. The sibling then goes to Dad and gets him onside. With the backing of you and Dad, the sibling approaches Mum to change her mind. That's politics.

OK that seems simple, but as you have learned already nothing in life is that simple. The next step is that Mum, after reluctantly giving in to letting the younger sibling go, then comes down with the rules.

You have to be accompanied by a parent.
Parents will take you there.
You have to come home directly after the concert.

So then you say you wanted to go with your friends, and while you didn't mind dragging the kid along, it would spoil the whole thing if a parent came as well.

The next step is that you start to put pressure on Dad to get Mum to back off and let the kid come with your friends on the train. Dad says it is starting to get too difficult and he wasn't that happy about the kid going in the first place. You storm off in a huff.

For the next week, you think of ways that you may be able to swing Mum around. You do the dishes, make your bed, keep your room tidy and then you are about to front Mum with what a responsible kid you are when your report card arrives in the mail and you got a bad report for attitude.

Dad hits the roof and pulls his support for the Adele concert, Mum says it was all off anyway because the kid wasn't going on the train and you have to retreat to your room because you can see it is a lost cause.

Welcome to politics. That is pretty much the way the politicians play around, they spend most their time playing politics, that is trying to enhance their ability to influence decision-making, and a small amount of time actually attending to the act of governing the state.

Political debate

A formal debate is supposed to occur when two sides discuss an issue. One side supports a resolution and the other side opposes it. There are rules to debate. Each side gets a time frame to make its argument, and the opposite side remains quiet while that argument is being made.

In politics, that is simply not happening. Neither side gets to make its points uninterrupted. But the worst behaviour that has made its way into political debate is one side gives an argument and the other side attacks the person that made the argument not the argument itself.

The left, especially, has formulated a process that the right has found impossible to break. Ben Shapiro outlines how to debate when people become personal, throw in red herrings and get you sucked into paradigms that on the surface nobody is going to argue against.

Taxation

For the type of taxes, history of taxation, individual taxes I refer you to Wikipedia.

Major arguments on tax have been going on forever and when we get to a tipping point like at Runnymede it is going to take many generations before the issues are settled. Having said that bloodshed can be avoided by starting the process.

As with every subject, there are a number of issues that need to be balanced regarding taxation.

How much?

Each year the government prepares a budget of what it is going to spend over the next four years. These are called the forward estimates. By looking at the budget, the government knows what it has budgeted to spend and it knows what taxes are likely to be collected, and that brings it to establishing whether it will be in surplus, earning more than it spends, or deficit, spending more than it earns.

Argument has raged for centuries on who should pay what. There are the two basic arguments. The capitalists say that if you want to collect more in the future you need to encourage people to earn more. That means encouraging industry. The socialist argue that it is not fair that the strong keep all the money. The wealthy need to pay more tax to look after those not as fortunate. The government of the time tries to work out how they can collect more money without offending too many of their voters. As a result, we come up with a tax act that has thousands of pages which nobody really understands. Every time the government finds a way of taxing more, the people being taxed find a way around paying that tax. And the game goes on.

Collection

The whole collection system is inefficient and unproductive. It employs thousands of people on both sides trying to figure out what that massive tax act really says. In the past, some politicians have suggested a flat tax either for income tax or a goods and services tax. The result of that is that the thousands of people that rely on the complexity of the tax act lobby the government against more simple taxes, and around the circle we go.

Government need

The amount of tax collected is a function of the needs of the government. Unfortunately, the governance system has got itself into a real problem. To stay in power, the government feels it needs to give people more so they will vote for them at the next election. It was published in April 2017 that 60% of Australian families pay no net income tax. Over 80% of retirees are on the pension and 25% of 18–24-year-olds have a major income from the government. Therefore, the government needs to progressively increase taxes to give more to the majority and the never-ending cycle has begun.

How efficient is the system?

The vast majority of the tax system is inefficient. That means that it actually costs more to collect the tax than the value of the tax collected. In May 2017, the argument for the collection of goods and services tax (GST) on imported goods under $1,000 was raging. If you order a $100 item online from overseas, it is not taxed. But if it were taxed, who would pay the tax, where would it be collected and what would the process be. Obviously for someone to note the item has come into Australia and send out an invoice for $10 would cost more than $10. Therefore, it would be an inefficient tax.

I would argue that most tax is inefficient. By the time you add the $3.5 billion per year to run the ATO with the much greater cost of tax agents, accountants and financial advisers, one has to wonder just how inefficient the system really has become.

For example the Banking Levy of 2017. If a bank made a profit of $1bill in 2016 it would pay 30% tax, that is $300 mill. The other $700mill would be paid as dividends to shareholders and reinvested to grow the business. After 2017 the government will levy the bank say $300mill. This reduces the profit to $700mill and therefore the bank tax to $210mill. If the bank paid out 80% of profits as dividends then pre 2017 the dividends would be $560mill and after 2017 $392mill. If all the dividends went to buy goods and services then the government would receive $56mill in GST pre 2017 and $39mill post 2017. These goods and services would boost the economy. Therefore pre 2017 for every $1bill in profit the government would receive $300mill in company tax, $70mill in GST, and have $700 mill injected into the economy to increase GDP. After 2017 the government collects $300mill in levies, $210mill in company tax, and $39mill in GST. The unthinking would say the government is $193mill better off. However the $549mill collected by the government goes into a welfare hole that generates nothing for the growth of the economy. The reality is that the new tax strips the economy of the capital it needs to grow in the future.

Later we will discuss how capital is replacing personal exertion as the principle source of wealth creation, and therefore the removal of capital from the economy in the form of taxes has a detrimental effect on future growth.

Singapore

Years ago the tax rate in Singapore was 18%. The government put the rate up to 20%. They collected less money. They put it back to 18% and regained their income. The more the government wants to tax those horrible wealthy people the more protective those people become. At 18% you pay. At 20% it is worth a fight.

The Economy

The economy is the state of the country in terms of the production and consumption of goods and services and the supply of money.

Wikipedia. "An economy is an area of the production, distribution, or trade and consumption of goods and services by different agents in a geographical location."

Investopedia. "The large set of inter-related production and consumption activities that aid in determining how scarce resources are allocated."

So the economy is all about production and consumption of goods and services. The size of the economy is measured by gross domestic product (GDP).

GDP is defined as the total value of goods produced and services provided during one year.

Skipping ahead for a minute. When we talk about our own economy or finances we will talk about wealth, where wealth is the accumulation of resources, meaning assets.

So the country does not measure assets, it measures the production of goods and services, and that is a major issue within our political and economic system.

The economy does not consider the ongoing utilisation of capital.

If a chief executive officer (CEO) came into a corporation and used all the company's capital to spend up big on consumables thereby draining the balance sheet they would be sacked in seconds. But in government, a treasurer can use all the country's capital for ventures that have no chance of returning on capital, and there is no issue.

Even the measure of the size of the economy is all wrong. GDP takes into account the monetary value of finished goods and services produced within the country's borders. This includes even non-value adding activities. When GDP was first brought in as a measure many economists thought that government services should not be included, I would go a step further and say that all non-value adding services should not be included, such as all the regulatory work carried out. If you really want to know the size of the economy you should measure that part of the economy that has value moving forward and not the processing of money around in circles.

Why is this important? The success or failure of the economy is measured in the value of GDP. If there are two quarters in which the economy contracts then we call it a recession and everybody gets really scared, hides their money under their bed and turns out the lights early. It is 25 years since Australia had a recession and there are two major reasons:

If the government thinks we are getting close to a recession it increases government spending and therefore economic activity. It is the equivalent of someone going broke going on a spending spree to give the impression they are not going broke.

You bring in 200,000 immigrants every year. They all need to be clothed and fed, this increases the consumption of goods and services and therefore GDP even if the GDP per capita is going down.

GDP is a really dumb measurement, but that is the one we have so we can kid ourselves we are doing a whole lot better than we really are.

The State of the Economy

A hundred years ago, it was said that Australia rode on the sheep's back. That is the main source of income was from the sale of wool. We then started to build a mining industry as well as wheat and cattle industries. Soon Australia was known as a farm and a quarry. After the second world war, we developed a manufacturing industry to support the mining and agricultural industries. We made farm machinery, steel, cars, rope, ladders all sorts of things. Air travel started in the 1960s. (Before that if you wanted to go to Europe or America you went by ship.) and this was followed by the importing of cheaper products from overseas.

Australia had tariffs which made the imported goods more expensive but in the 1970s the theoretical economists convinced the government that it was much fairer to drop the tariffs and use all our money to buy cheap goods from overseas. This was called economic rationalism and it meant that the Australia manufacturer slowly went out of business from the 1980s through to now.

Because of economic rationalism or globalisation, Australia now has an economy that looks like this:

Total GDP: $1.7 trillion

Government, Federal and State	36%
Mining	12%
Agriculture	10%
Finance	12%
Manufacturing	6%
Construction	21%
International Tourism	0.2%
International Education	0.1%
Regulatory	11%

Now you will notice that this adds up to more than 100%, but you have to remember that there is plenty of red tape in government and the federal government contribution is 36% and some of that money then moves through the state governments and is counted again.

Having said all that these are still very scary figures and should have all of you being very afraid for the future of the Australian economy.

If we break down the figures:

Mining adds value to the economy, great.

Agriculture adds value to the economy, another big tick.

Manufacturing has gone from 14% in 1974 to 6% in 2015 and continues to decline.

Finance simply moves money around in circles, it produces nothing and adds no value to the assets of the nation.

Construction is nice to have in order that we have great places to live and work, but it is not like buying a machine that is going to create output for you in the future.

Tourism and education have been touted by the Greens as parts of the economy that are going to take over from manufacturing but they are going to need massive growth to get anywhere near the 14% of GDP we gave away.

Australia's GDP is about $1.7 trillion. Mining, agriculture and manufacturing are the wealth creation centres representing 28% of GDP. Construction takes the capital produced from mining, agriculture and manufacturing and turns it into capital in the form of bricks and mortar. Government, finance and red tape represent what is known these days as the transactional costs and education and tourism are the so-called emerging industries.

So economic rationalism morphed into globalisation has wiped out 8% of GDP and replaced it with red tape and finance both non-value-adding activities.

Companies

We have seen that Australia is still a farm and a quarry but it gets worse.

We all know that the world is changing at a rapid rate. Industries are moving on, yet look at the ASX50 mostly old companies at the end of their lifespan. The Dow Jones is packed with FAANG, Facebook, Amazon, Apple, Netflix and Google. It even gets scarier when we get into the private sector. Most large family businesses have moved away from their original business and become developers. That is, they have moved out of manufacturing and into construction. Those that have stayed in their original businesses have moved overseas where the business climate is more user friendly.

Superimposed on that scenario is that the new US President has identified these issues and is taking steps to move US capital back onshore, build new manufacturing capacity in the US and reduce the impediments to doing business in the US.

I will emphasise here that in discussions with the federal government over many years I put it forward that the cost of labour in Australia is not the big issue it is the distribution chain that is the issue.

Retailers have their paradigms and do not try to work outside them. In the shoe industry in 1970 a shoe used to sell for three times its manufacturing cost, today it sells for more than 14 times the manufacturing cost. That means the cost of manufacturing is between 7 and 8% of the retail price. You could double the cost of manufacturing and it would still only be 15% of the retail price.

Quick response manufacturing required attention to information systems and to logistics were all too hard for the retail industry and as a result we lost a perfectly good manufacturing base that employed many of the newer immigrants that were in the middle of the language learning curve.

Corporate culture

Seventy-five years ago, an economist named Joseph Schumpeter predicted that when corporations become bureaucracies run by executives rather than hungry entrepreneurs, capitalism will have planted the seeds of its own destruction. Later the changes in the boardroom have been discussed in relation to outsourcing. Here we need to discuss the role of the board in relation to the economy and the community.

Corporations have been dragged into social issues as well as economic ones. The question is, has the line been crossed when the CEOs of major corporations write to the prime minister saying "Enabling loving, committed couples to be married, regardless of their sexual orientation, will contribute to a stronger economy and more inclusive Australia." That statement could be debated on so many levels.

Whatever your belief is, what has gay marriage got to do with the strength of the economy? And how is allowing gay marriage making Australia more inclusive? One has to wonder how and why the CEOs of 35 of Australia's largest companies got around to signing such a letter. More to the point is how many refused to sign it. Why does the signature of a corporate CEO carry more weight than yours or mine? Who did the research and who paid for it? But it all comes down to corporate culture.

In recent times there have been a few deviations from traditional corporate culture. The first was the Board of Cricket Australia when they gave into their players and effectively lost control of a significant portion of their P&L. This cultural change surfaced again only a few months later when the Australian cricket team felt that it was OK to cheat. The same cultural changes have occurred in the major banks and financial institutions where it appears it was seen as OK to charge for services not delivered.

Once upon a time, the board drew up the mission and vision for the company and then employed a CEO to reach the targets set. Now the board outsources the visionary stuff to the CEO's who apparently have taken it upon themselves to run the corporation in the shadow of their own personal beliefs often contrary to those of their customers, suppliers and shareholders.

Here comes the end of capitalism. When the CEOs of major companies choose to speak out on controversial social change yet make no comment of the sombre economic future ahead, we have a problem.

Summary

Australia has returned to its roots of being a farm and a quarry. The government continues to put imposts on those sections of the economy that add wealth. The result is that we have technically had three recessions in the last ten years. The economy is going backwards in relation to GDP and productivity per capita and the country is being hoodwinked by a political process that is incapable of selling the facts for what they are.

The most disturbing statistic is the number of new businesses that add growth to the economy. The barriers to entry have risen well above risk tolerance levels on two fronts. The first is that it is impossible for a small start-up without major backing to get the accreditation and certification that it needs to join the party. The second is that disruptive businesses are having such a massive effect on corporations that growth is not guaranteed for any business. Traditionally strong and energetic young people would borrow to fund their long-term dreams. These days dreams are not long-term and therefore people are reticent to borrow capital to put into a business that may not be around for long. The example of Amazon shows how a massive company can be built on projected income and not capital.

A decade of extravagant spending has left the Australian economy with a huge debt to carry. But worse still there is a budget that is never likely to return to surplus and a welfare bill that is gaining momentum every day. The demographics are changing and more and more people are requiring welfare.

Australia has come to a crisis point; the question is when that point will be recognised.

The Economic Debate

The economic debate between the socialists and the capitalists is much greater than just the concept of equality or fairness as it has been dubbed.

The economic debate is about the economic pie. The focus of the capitalists is to increase the size of the economy. They believe that to survive you have to grow. The world is growing at an extra 100 million mouths per year. Australia is growing at an extra 350,000 mouths per year. Unless the economy grows, then we all go backwards.

As we saw before there are millions of people every year coming out of poverty. Those people have to produce more to feed and clothe themselves.

So we have the capitalists wanting to use capital to build productive assets such as roads, dams, bridges, airports, factories and mines. The job of capital is to produce a return. Increase the return on the capital and there is more to go around. Increase the size of the pie and everybody can have more.

The socialists believe that the job of the government is to share around what is already there. Capital is used for consumables. After the money is spent it has gone and there is no more left behind.

This is no different to the choices you are going to face. There was an adage that said a 20-year-old that buys a new car will at the age of 30 have a ten-year-old car. The 20-year-old that buys a house will have at 30 a house and a car. It is as simple as that and at the end of the course you will understand how it happens.

But as far as the debate is concerned you have the capitalists talking in a language of growth, rates of return, future income. And you have the socialist speaking in the language of fairness, need and equality. The languages are so different that both sides do not even understand what the other side is saying let alone understand the concepts and ideas behind the language.

The point

Why do you need to understand economics? The answer is that you live in a far more complex world than your parents. Technology, politics and culture are changing at a rate never seen before. The economy is what we are in relation to finance. How do we make our money, and where do we spend it? The economy will be greatly influenced by politics, religion and culture. Changes will occur that affect you and you need to make your changes, not wait and change later or indeed wonder what happened later.

In 2015, major super funds were invested 10% in international shares, three years later that is 35%. There are reasons for that change and you need to know about them.

As a nation, we are racking up debt that will have to be paid off in the future. We have thrown away our manufacturing industries and have no jobs for the people that used to work in those industries. We are relying on the growth of new industries that nobody can define or identify. As a nation, we have jumped off one slippery rock and are about to land on the next slippery rock.

I was studying in London in 1976. I had all my money in a bank account in Australian dollars and didn't have my finger on the pulse. I arrived in London in September 1976 and had enough money to live until the end of the course in September 1977. On 28 November 1976, the Australian government devalued the $A by 17.5%. I lost 17.5% of the money I had to live on for the next year. Had I been on the ball I would have known something was going on and transferred the money to English pounds. Big mistake.

Now you are probably going to say that your parents didn't know this stuff when they were your age. That is why I am trying to explain the size of the changes to population, the speed of the changes to technology and the depth of the changes to politics and culture. One hundred years ago your life expectancy was so low you didn't need a plan. Now with the ground moving under you and the length of the new race you had better have a plan, and to make that plan you had better have a great understanding of the political, financial, cultural and physical environment in which you live.

Culture

Culture is the ideas, customs and social behaviour of a particular people or society.

Australia as I would like to know it is a unified culture started when the first fleet arrived. There was the indigenous culture and the British culture. They were miles apart but they managed to coexist. We will discuss immigration later, but for now let's look at the different cultures that have come to make up the multi-ethnic society that today is Australia. First there were the Chinese, followed by Northern Europeans, Eastern Europeans, and the Western Europeans. There were major influxes of Indians, Vietnamese and later Africans. So many cultures and so many religions.

Australia has taken a little from each culture that came here and defined its own culture for over one hundred years. It has been a natural process. When a new culture arrives the existing population step back and look at the new arrivals, then they go up and start communication, often the reply is not understood and they step back

In Australia, this used to happen because of language difficulties. The immigrants did not speak the language and therefore they tend to stick together in their safe environment. Their children started to go to school and learned the new language and before long, all the children had integrated. This resulted eventually in mixed marriages and mixed cultures. The integration of cultures is not an Australian thing, it is a world thing. John Lennon spoke of it in "Imagine" as have many other artists. Remember one hundred years ago there were only 1.7 billion people on the planet and aeroplanes did not exist.

The world has changed so fast and we expect that we can change with it, well we cannot. It is going to take time to develop a fully integrated culture and that is if all the participants actually want it.

Psychology

Psychology is the scientific study of the human mind and its functions, especially those affecting behaviour in a context.

There has been much written about psychology in a whole range of different areas from business to love. There is no doubt psychology is an incredibly important part of your life and your environment. It will help you immensely if you can understand how you think and how others think. It is important that we put the function of our human mind into context. Modern humans, known as *Homo sapiens*, diverged from *Homo neanderthalensis* about 500,000 years ago. Since then, there have been a number of major changes to lifestyles that require a change to our psychology. What we do need to be aware of is the rate of change. It took over 500,000 years from the control of fire to the introduction of the electric light, but only another 100 years before the electric light turned into an electronic tablet.

Thought patterns and positive mental attitude (PMA)

Because of the lifestyle 500,000 years ago the main thoughts were negative. Life was short and you had to be on your toes the whole time. Danger was around every corner. As a result, the mind was bombarded with negative thoughts every minute of every day. I can imagine a child being counselled in those days about playing in the woods because of the lurking dangers. Fast forward to today when children are sent to psychologists to rid themselves of negative thoughts and replace them with positive ones.

By nature, we have developed over a million years, not an exaggeration, a thought pattern based on our radar, sonar and ultrasound detectors that tries to identify dangers and possible dangers. This inbuilt system is with us all the time. I have read we all have over 45,000 negative thoughts per day. That is one every 2 seconds. At the same time, we are told to feel good about ourselves. Just great, I am going to overcome my inbuilt defensive system of negative thoughts.

We have developed many ways of driving out these negative thoughts. Things like music, PlayStation, YouTube, alcohol and sex all come to mind. You need to understand what you are doing with your negative thoughts and how you are dealing with them. If you find and external solution like those just mentioned you will have great difficulties because as your brain becomes accustomed to the distraction, it will require more of the same distraction to rid yourself of those thoughts.

The power of these negative thoughts has been used as punishment for centuries. One of the ultimate tortures is sensory deprivation. Put someone in solitary confinement for days at a time dealing with only their own thoughts and see what happens.

There is a difference between overcoming your fears and numbing your negative thoughts with external painkillers.

So the concept of positive mental attitude (PMA) was born. Focus your mind on the positive and put those negatives thoughts away each day. Let me tell you, that can be really tiring. While some people may believe in PMA others believe in focusing on goals, others believe in natural stimulants and others in artificial stimulants. The point is that your body is programmed through hundreds of thousands of years of evolution to put those negative thoughts in your mind each day. I notice it when I am living on a boat. You hear every little noise, you feel every little vibration and you notice every little change in light. When your life depends on it you notice these little things. When living in caves or out in the open the human mind became tuned into their environment to a point where they learned to look after themselves in the company of predators and many creatures that were just trying to defend themselves.

Natural Methods

Over a period, we have developed many natural methods of getting over this anxiety of having negative thoughts. The three most popular appear to be sex, eating and exercise. All three are complicated because they actually all have natural functions as well. We needed to have sex to procreate and we required to exercise to hunt and gather. But whether through evolution or creation we got a bonus for procreating, it feels good. The same thing for the hunter and gatherer. When running to get food and being put in scary situations by the animals you are hunting, you need a boost and that comes in the form of adrenalin and endorphins. Now the problem is that in hunting and gathering and procreating we decided this could be good fun and would also hide our negative thoughts.

Unnatural Methods

Humans have developed many unnatural ways of putting the demons to rest. Music was probably the first followed closely by alcohol and the two in combination can completely wipe out the negative thoughts. However, if you do not get in control of your negative thoughts you are likely to find that you need more and more alcohol and music. When that is not enough you turn to other drugs, interactive games, YouTube and watching 20 episodes of your favourite TV series at a single sitting.

The point of all this is that over the last 500,000 years your mind has evolved to deal with the environment in which it lived. That environment has changed dramatically over the last century, and to be fair we just haven't allowed the physiology of the brain to catch up with our environmental evolution. The result is that our minds are still doing the jobs they were trained for all those years ago, but there is no reason to be constantly searching for the threats that used to be around. We therefore need to understand that we have this machine in our heads generating one negative thought every two seconds and we have to adapt to it. Feeling those negative thoughts are a normal function of our brain, you will never suppress the negative thoughts so you need to learn to live with them. There are many ways of doing that you need to find the one that works for you.

Remember that too much food, alcohol, exercise, adrenalin or sex is an indication that you are not on the right path to dealing with those negative thoughts.

Why is it that so many kids are being diagnosed with ADHD, or adolescents are seeking psychological help? The answer could be that we are dealing with a new environment without a new brain.

Language

Language has evolved over thousands of years and will no doubt continue to evolve. There are any number of factors driving our changes to language.

Technology

Mobile phones and technology have had a significant effect on our language. We now say many things in shorthand and use emojis to transfer our thoughts. We are all aware of the Chinese whispers game where one person whispers a message to another and this goes on down a line of ten to 20 people. The message that comes out the other end can be very different than the one put in. The same occurs in shorthand messages. I have been in many conversations by text or email, and often they end up in a total misunderstanding of what is being said.

Fashion

Words have been made up for fashionable reasons for centuries, however now we are putting significantly different meanings on a single word. When my grandkids tell me I look sick, I didn't get that was a good thing. Apparently sick is awesome or Ab Fab as opposed to unwell. It is easy to see how fashion changes in words can cause issues. When you first go to America you think they speak English only to learn they do not. My wife was looked at in horror when she arrived at a cousin's house and asked if she could nurse the baby. We are often nations separated by a common language.

Cultural wars

In the 1980s Social History, which concentrates on the social, economic and cultural institutions of people morphed into Cultural History which concentrates on the environmental history of a species focusing on race, class, gender and sexuality. This trait was accelerated by the advent of social media in 2007.

Before that time an academic had to have their ideas peer reviewed before being published. However social media made it easier for academics to find other academics throughout the world that could peer review their work and therefore it was much easier for fringe concepts to get published.

These cultural wars started the concept of speech repression and grew into concepts such as linguistic constructivism and postmodernism.

The explanation of the above is that a number of academics developed the belief, notice I said belief and not theory, that truth was a function of human consensus and could not be measured scientifically. Let's translate into today's language. If you say something long and loud enough then people will believe it. And that, my friends, has been the thrust of the cultural changes over the last century. It is not important that what you are saying is correct, it is just important that enough people believe it and then by nature it is correct. Now if I was to put that to most rational human beings they would think I had gone crazy, but that is how we live in our culture today. Whether it be advertising or politics we are told what others want to be the truth, we are not told the truth. One of our biggest issues as a culture is that the vast majority of journalists went to these schools and believe their role is to make you believe what they write. It is not their aim to report the truth, as they would like it to be, it is their aim to invent the truth and then sell it.

Linguistic Constructivism became the concept that we construct the world by language, and even corporations started to use the language. A Nike slogan from the 1990s "We are the stories we tell."

Politicians started to use communications to define the world as they wanted us to see it. The Labor Party did it very effectively with fairness and Mediscare.

As a result, we moved to changing the words we were allowed to utter in relation to race, gender, class and sexuality. Much of the language was forbidden. I remember at school learning about the reformation when soldiers went around Europe burning books. I have to confess as a teenager in the sixties I had not thought of the consequences. They had no radio and no trains therefore no books meant no learning. The thoughts of an entire religion and generation were destroyed.

In climate change, the conservationist strongholds were infiltrated and taken over by the preservationists. In language, the guardians were taken over by academics using social media and bullying tactics to remove words in relation to class, gender, racism and sexuality from the language. So now with laws such as Section 18C of the *Racial Discrimination Act* you can be sued for using these words that were a normal part of speech only a decade ago. The Labor Party has in it policies that Section 18C will be expanded from just racial words to words in relation to gender, class and sexuality.

Remember the definition of socialism included the democratic control of political ideologies and theories. Free speech was the basis of our democratic system. Socialism has not just tried but has succeeded in destroying free speech in Australia. The law has taken over the power to tell you what you can and what you cannot say.

But this change in language hasn't solved the issues at stake. What it has done is to drive these issues underground. We do not use racists language in public anymore therefore we are not racist. The same effect is seen in climate science. There are many words you are not allowed to say and therefore you cannot argue against the prescribed theories, so by definition the prescribed theories must be correct.

Summary

Social engineering of language has stopped debate on the many subjects we need to debate to move our culture forward. Political correctness has the aim of shaping our thoughts by controlling language. The thought control police started to control the public through Universities, Bureaucracies and the mainstream political media. They are now moving into the community framing what can and cannot be debated in public.

Communication

Our communications these days are so much better than they were in the past. Semaphore and Morse Code were replaced by radios, radar replaced look outs, HF radio went around the world and then came the age of the telephone followed by satellites and sat phones. Today we have hand held devices that not only make phone calls and tell the time but allow contact with the rest of the world through the internet. The technology of communications has increased dramatically. However, I question whether the accuracy of communications is any better than it was before the telephone was invented. At least in the days of the telegraph people thought very carefully about the words they used as they were paying by the word. Today people whack out an SMS or a tweet without thinking too much and then there it is for life. In the days of letter writing when you wrote a letter in anger the rule of thumb was to put it in a drawer for 48 hours before posting it. The theory being that if you still felt offended or peeved off after 2 days then go ahead. Most times you tore up the letter and moved on. The Moody Blues immortalised the words in Nights in White Satin. "Letters I've written never meaning to send." people got their feelings out on paper and then destroyed the paper. Psychologists caught onto this and had people in pain write about it and then they had ritual burnings of the hurtful material. Today all that seems to have gone out the window and people react immediately to threats and reply on social media. Perhaps some of the old ways weren't that bad after all.

I have been critical of younger generations because they seem to think that you can communicate as well through technology as you can one on one face to face. It has been shown time and again that in face to face discussion 80% of the communication is nonverbal. Body language, eyes and even aura carry most of the communication. The argument for not having face to face meetings seems to be around cost. But I would argue it is more about lifestyle. It is not fun traveling around the world or even the country meeting with people to do the business or get the job done. It definitely is more pleasant being in your comfortable lifestyle at home. Being able to go to the footy on the weekends or meet with your mates during the week. Tucking the kids up for the night instead of yet another dinner with people who speak in different tongues. The question is to the efficiency of getting the communication correct versus the cost of the travel to get it right.

Having said that meeting people eye to eye and seeing the works on the ground gets conveyed through the eye of the beholder. I wonder at how military leaders made decisions before satellite communications. There was a need to take the words and also understand the person that was conveying those words. My admiration for field generals rose immensely after cyclone Yasi. We were held up in Townsville because the road was closed trying to get back to Cardwell where our home had been damaged in a category 5 cyclone.

The first rule of communications was broken at the road block. We were trying to find out the situation with the roads and there was no mobile reception. However, the police had sat phones so we thought we were in. Firstly, the police had not been trained in how to use the phone and secondly, they wouldn't let us civilians have a go. So we tripped back to Townsville where we got three reports on our house.

Report number one said. Leave your wife back in Townsville get a truck and some young men and come and collect the few things that remain before leaving the house for good.

The second report was that things didn't seem too bad. The gen set seemed OK and we should be OK to return although the house was a mess.

The third report said there was little or no damage and the house had made it through the night looking good.

A little perplexed we drove back the next day via the development road. 8 hours instead of one and a half. We arrived to find that the water had gone through the house to the depth of about 150mm leaving about 5mm of sediment as it left. The front garden was in the living room and furniture had been flung all over the place. So how did this equate with the three reports we had. The first report was from an emotional man in his 70s looking at the mud and the ruined furniture, all he could see was devastation. The second was an electrician so I was surprised that he hadn't seen that in fact the gen set had been in the garage and was completely covered with water. The third was a builder and he couldn't see any damage because he was looking past the mess and looking only at the structure. We had lost a bit of roof and a few gutters but nothing else that mattered in his eyes.

In retrospect, each of the reports was correct in the eyes of the beholder. You needed to be a magician on the other end of the phone to interpret.

Communication is as much about how you receive it as how you give it, which is why I still prefer face to face if you want to get it right.

Moving on that point to another level it is important to understand just where your listener is at. Some years ago, I was trying to get a message through to the grandchildren and I could see I was getting nowhere. I related the story to a daughter in law who said "The message doesn't get through if the receiver isn't on". How true.

Negotiation

Cultural differences come through in negotiating styles and it is important to understand them. After a few trips to China I was told that the Chinese got on well with the Australians and that was a big advantage for us in negotiations. I was then told the story of a big American company that was trying to negotiate a deal with a Chinese SOE. A meeting was set up and the Chinese felt it would take about 3 days to get through the agenda. The day before the meeting the president of the American company flew in on his company jet, followed a few hours later by about 3 vice presidents. The main body of the negotiators came in on commercial airlines. All the attendees gathered the next morning and the Americans sat around the table waiting for the meeting to start. The Chinese were standing around waiting to greet their guests.

With the Americans taking control the meeting started and the president kicked off with the items he needed to go through. As soon as he had finished his items he got on his plane and flew back to the states. The same thing happened the next day with each of the VPs in turn. By lunch on the third day the whole of the Chinese team was still there but only a couple of American interns remained at the table. The Americans had fulfilled their agenda. It was at this time that the Chinese asked their questions and there was nobody there that understood the issues let alone knew how to deal with them. The Chinese leave their most important issues to the last, whereas the Americans start with the biggest issue and work down the list. The other difference is that the Chinese want to meet you and dine with you before the meeting. It is about the relationship for them. So why do Australians go so well? The Australians do not mind going out for dinner and drinking huge quantities of alcohol for days on end before it is time to get down to business. Australians are willing to build the relationship, and that is the important point. It is not just about language it is about customs and social behaviour.

Regulation

Although regulation is an important part of our governance and economy it has also become such a significant part of our culture. Regulations have become a major part of our ideas, customs and social behaviour. I remember a fellow student while I was doing an MBA talking about a backyard BBQ. He was a very bright engineer with a young family. The parents were standing around talking and rolling sausages on the BBQ when one father went right off at his son. The eight-year-old boy had picked up a bike and was riding around the backyard on the lawn without his helmet. My friend who was brought up in rural Tasmania couldn't believe what he was hearing. Sure, helmets on the road but in the backyard. Our discussion went further. Have kids lost their six sense for danger? Today there is a sign put up for every danger, do the kids understand where there may be danger if there is no sign? So the question remains, has helicopter parenting been responsible for the loss of ability to detect danger?

Legislators haven't got it yet. You cannot regulate out poor behaviour. The regulations will get tighter and tighter until there will be a cessation of ideas and our social behaviour will become so withdrawn that realistic communication will be denied.

In our culture regulations have taken over from common sense. There was a great example after cyclone Yasi. A few days after the cyclone when we had the houses cleaned and things were starting to get back to a sort of norm. No water and no power though, the council thought it was time to clean the roads and public places.

There was a shortage of drivers so I volunteered to drive one of the trucks. We all got our orders from the council the night before. It clearly stated that we should not bring tailgates. So the tailgates were taken off the trucks and each excavator was allocated a couple of trucks. The excavator loaded the trucks with debris and the trucks delivered it to the Cardwell dump.

Now, Cardwell was a town of 1,400 people before the cyclone, and 800 after. Not a big town, not a big dump. There were 20 trucks working. Having a numeric mind, I started doing the maths. We were dumping at the rate of one truck every 45 secs. The locations were moving as we filled up the dump, the ground was wet and muddy and there were a couple of big bulldozers and an excavator in there with us feeding the giant mulching machine. There were two dumping spots, sometimes three.

It is hard to imagine the activity in that little muddy pit literally hundreds of tons of machinery driven by thousands of horsepower moving over a thousand tons of broken foliage every hour. This was all being achieved by drivers and operators with an average age well over 60 years of age. It was fun to be a part of such a professional team of drivers and operators. The excavator drivers knew how to load trucks and even though the streets were strewn with debris. I never saw anything flying off a moving vehicle. All was going well and the clean-up looked like it would be all over in a couple of days.

At four o'clock that afternoon the regulatory police arrived in town with their bright green vests all fresh faced. It took them ten minutes to pull over the first driver and book him for driving without tailgates along a public road. The police and the council tried to explain but the fresh faced regulatory crew stuck to their guns. We were all told that night to put the tailgates back on. So off to work the next day and I measured that instead of one truck dumping every 45 secs it was one every 150 seconds. In addition, it required us old men to get out of the cabs, unhook loads caught by the gates and also open and close the gates. It was dangerous and inefficient. It was 24 loads per hour instead of 80 loads. It was insane and to me it has stuck in my mind as an example of where we have gone so wrong.

Work to regulations has always been known to bring a site to a grinding halt, here I was in the middle of it watching productivity plummet.

This event occurred through a number of failures. The first was a governance failure. In the same period after cyclone Larry, Peter Cosgrove was installed in Innisfail to run the clean-up. He had the authority to make his own emergency rules. In that case, there were no tailgates for a week, and no covers for the next week. Then things got back to normal and the covers went back on. But Yasi was straight on top of the Brisbane floods and the operation was being run out of Brisbane with no eyes or ears on the ground. Common sense did not prevail. There was a massive economic failure. 80 loads per hour went to 24 loads per hour that is 640 loads per day down to 192. A 70% reduction in productivity. It was taking three times as long to do the same job. In fact, instead of having the job finished in a few days it took weeks to complete at a cost four times what it should have been. The cost of course being borne by the ratepayers.

Today we know that this occurs on a daily basis. It is well documented that government construction costs three times what it would if it were you or me. This has been our way. Regulations are shattering ideas, changing our customs and our social behaviour to the point that productivity is no longer an aim of our society. Just remember from our work on economics if the economy does not grow it dies, and ours is dying because we as a society do not care.

Social Behaviour

The whole concept of social behaviour has changed in the last century mainly for economic and technical reasons. Why is this important for you the know? It is not so important that you know what has happened but it is important that you are aware of the changes. It is like the story of the frog in the boiling water. Social behaviour has changed dramatically but is that good or bad. You need to know the history in order to judge for yourself whether you are going in the wrong or right direction.

We have established that a century ago most people worked to live. Therefore, life was pretty much get up go to work come home feed and sleep and then do it all again. As things got better there would be social events on the weekend and perhaps trips during a holiday. Dining out was a very special event and if you wanted a cup of coffee you sat around the kitchen table. The advent of the telephone, it wasn't that long ago, changed the situation entirely. Now kids that spent all day at school together could also spend the night on the phone.

Then the smart phone and the internet came along, which dragged along Facebook behind it.

All these changes have opened our society in every way. Because we are Skyping, FaceTiming, Facebooking or sending selfies we get to see each other all the time. From climbing out of bed in the morning to getting back in at night nothing seems to be sacred. We all know what each other eats, drinks, thinks and does. That means that when we get together for a coffee or a pizza then there is nothing to talk about, so we spend the time on the phone to someone else so that when we see them face to face there will be nothing to talk about.

I used to love going to the cricket, nothing better than the boxing day test after a hard year at work. The last time I went with a bunch of people there was no sitting and watching the cricket it was getting up to meet other people, going for a drink or eats or just spending time on the phone Facebooking. You do not need to watch the cricket because when something happens it will be replayed on the big screen, followed by a replay in the bar and endless replays available on your phone. It is hard to understand why they go there at all.

Dressing has changed. The girls still seem to go to a lot of trouble to look good, having said that I have noticed that they seem more interested in looking good for their female friends rather than any males they may meet. The boys just seem to not care or have any idea of what is reasonable behaviour. You only have to sit next to a huge man in a singlet on a plane to grasp what I am trying to say. The whole social thing seems to be about me and not my interaction with others.

One of the major changes to social behaviour has been in the use of alcohol. The use of alcohol was a lot more intergenerational than it is now. Whether that is a good thing or not I am not sure. What I do know is that certain standards have changed and changed for the better. In my last year at school, all the year twelves were called into the assembly hall for, I guess you would call it a lecture, by the police surgeon. The talk was funny at times, tragic at other times but I will never forget the introduction. "Have a look to your left, then look to your right, one of you three will die in a car crash in the next 5 years." In 1970, 3,798 people lost their lives on the road out of a population of 12.5m. That is 1 in 3,300 people. In 2016, 1,290 people lost their lives on the road out of a population of 23million. That is one in every 18,800 people. What a massive change. Now there are many factors that affect that statistic, but it is one the nation should be proud of.

Social behaviour as part of our DNA

For 200 years' immigrants have taken huge risks to walk away from their homes and come here to build new lives for themselves and their families. They have learned a new language, new customs and have worked hard to build the life they were looking for. So what happened? The answer can be told in the Rags to Rags in three generations story.

This story has been told a thousand times, but it has particular relevance here. The first generation were fierce entrepreneurs, they worked hard. However, with that came the fact that they were single minded, obstinate and dictatorial. The result was that not only did they work hard but they put huge pressure on the next generation to work hard. At the same time, they were very strict with the next generation and had little time to spend with their children while they were growing up. If the children wanted to become their own people they were pushed back by the patriarch or matriarch and told to get on with it.

The result was that this new generation were a lot better off than their parents but they had the stuffing knocked out of them by the time they had any real control. This second generation was brought up in a vacuum of power yet with the wealth that their parents had created. They knew how to work hard, but their spirit had been broken by years of subservience. The second generation let their children run riot, they had wealth beyond their belief and could lavish education and lifestyle upon their children. The third generation having been totally pampered and never having to really work only knew how to spend, not how to earn. As they burnt through their families' wealth they turned to the state to provide for the habits they had acquired.

On the surface, it has become evident that the children and grandchildren of those hard-working motivated immigrants have been reliant on state welfare and have adopted the mentality of oppression. These people spend their lives in retreat, cannot stand up for themselves and automatically look for support.

I was involved in a debate at lifeline during a weekend conference. On one side were three business owners on the other side were three professional counsellors with degrees in psychology. We got about half way into the debate when the opposing speaker lay down on the floor prostrate. While lying there he spoke of how utterly defenseless he felt in the wake of our arguments. How can you imagine the son of people who had risked their life to travel half way around the world for a new life prostrating themselves in the face of a few words from people they had just shared lunch with? And that is why I fear for the future of our country. We were built from very strong stock whether it be the indigenous who have lived in this cruel country for millenniums, the descendants of convicts or the first free settlers looking for a new home, those fleeing either religious or racial persecution, or those just plain looking for a better future. How did their descendants stoop to the point of planning on how to make the most of the state welfare on offer?

One hope came in William. H. Overholt's book. When speaking of the Russians and Chinese coming out of communism he also spoke of their cultures. When the Russian oligarchs wanted to build new factories or infrastructure they would go to the peasants and tell them they had to move. The peasants would fight to stay in the hovels in which they lived. The Russian people had been suppressed all their lives either under a monarchy, communism or oligarchy. They had no will and no appetite for change. Their mindset was that a change always led to a future worse than the one they were in and therefore they resisted change at every turn. The Chinese on the other hand have a natural entrepreneurial flare. They think things will always get better. So when the government went along to thousands of people to say they had to move because the Three Gorges project was going to flood their towns, the people couldn't wait to get out. They packed up their belongings and were ready to move months before they had to go.

So when the government came to these people and said, you are no longer communists, you can now own land and be entrepreneurial, they jumped at the chance. This was a whole civilisation that had been suppressed for generations, which suddenly grew wings and flew. I remember visiting factories in China filled with workers about 20 years of age. These workers had no education and had been living in huts with earthen floors. Yet within weeks they were wearing knock offs of the latest New York fashions. The Chinese are a truly entrepreneurial people, it is in their DNA.

I can only hope that the Australian public will rise above the entitlement mentality and revert to being the self-sufficient nation builders that their ancestors were.

Research

When I was starting out in business I went to a lecture. In those days there were no conferences, or seminars there were lectures where you went along to get information from an expert in a field. As opposed to going to a conference where most people go to show everybody else how brilliant they are. Anyway, I went along to this lecture about technology in the future. This was in the late 1970s and computers did not exist in the workplace or in the place of study. If you wanted to know something you went to an encyclopaedia or a reference book to get the information.

So this industry leader gets up and starts telling us that in 1975 the hardest thing for a manager is to find enough information to make a decision. Then he goes on to say that by the year 2000 the biggest job for a manager will be sifting through masses of information and picking out the correct bits to make a decision. Of course in 1975 the guy was considered raving mad, by the year 2000 Rupert Murdoch was proven correct.

Computers have changed the way we do everything including research. The major issues with computers and research have been dealt with in other sections. The main point to remember is that it is important to set up a research process before you start playing with computer models. Use the computer as a tool and not as some sort of AI that is going to lead you to the answer.

Customs

All the different cultures around the world built up customs over many years. These customs defined a traditional and widely accepted way of behaving. In the European culture, there were customs of opening doors for women, addressing people by their titles, not commencing a meal before the hostess, seating ladies first at a table, taking your hat off when indoors and we could go on forever. In other cultures, there were or are a very different set of customs.

These days these customs have either been dispensed with or have been redefined. The traditional handshake has been completely redefined, but the opening of doors for women has been dispensed with completely. The minority groups in society want us all to be equal. It is outrageous that a man should be courteous to a woman, that is tantamount to saying she is not his equal in today's world. Of course for some women, there is the saying. "Why would I want to be equal with a man and have to lower myself to his level?"

Being a really old-fashioned conservative, I miss a lot of the old customs. The one I miss most is having respect for the title.

It doesn't matter if it is parents or the prime minister I miss the formality of the title. I find it obnoxious when a reporter asks a question of the prime minister addressing him or her by their first name. I know we are all equal and there is a real need to drag down the power of the title, however I still get uncomfortable when people in power are degraded. Even in the communist system it started out as Comrade, and moved to Comrade Name, and then moved to Comrade Title. Even in the communist system the leader would be called "Comrade President" and not by just their first name.

The dissolution of customs has taken away the framework of society. There is no longer any structure. Somebody told me that less than 10% of Australian families eat together at least once a day. The meal table used to be where stories were told. Achievements related and wounds healed. No longer do we sit and talk, we watch TV or YouTube, or text our friends. Maybe that is a reason we have lost the art of debate.

The customs of old created a framework and structure to our lives.

As immigrants came to our country they all brought with them their own traditions and customs. The poor ones died and the good ones were assimilated into the multi-ethnic society. We started to build up a concoction of customs that were becoming our own. But recent trends to equalise all members of society have waved the customs of old. Yet the newer immigrants are wishing to hold onto their customs, and now that we have released ours, there are no multicultural customs; there are theirs and none. Nature abhors a vacuum, so in the absence of a social structure a new one will form.

Groupthink

No discussion of the ideas and social behaviour today would be complete without dealing with groupthink which is the practice of thinking or making decisions as a group, resulting typically in unchallenged, poor quality decision-making. If we take the individual elements of group think we in fact have our politicians, academics and media of today. They hunt in groups, rarely does anyone stand out except on the other side. The consensus is never challenged or more to the point the consensus is never allowed to be challenged

The term groupthink was coined by Irving Evans in 1972. He said that it occurs when a group makes faulty decisions because group pressures lead to a deterioration of "mental efficiency, reality testing, and moral judgment".

I am sure you have been in groups when decisions have been made to do outrageous things especially when alcohol or euphoria have been in the mix. Young groups egg each other on to do things they would never do alone.

However now we have minority activist groups, politicians and even the CEOs of major companies being caught up in behaviour that would be seen as ridiculous if it were viewed in the light of mental efficiency, with thorough reality testing and a strong moral judgment.

These are all things you need to keep in mind when dealing with your political social and economic environment. Look at how others make decisions and do not get caught up in the global group think.

The legal system and culture

After discussing groupthink, it is important to relate that to the legal system in this country. Over the last few decades there has been a significant change that needs to be acknowledged and observed, and then reversed.

The first change was the movement from you are innocent until proven guilty. The way the system works at present is that anybody, at a small cost, can sue somebody else. And that person or entity that is sued is responsible for proving their innocence before the matter is ended. It has become known as punishment by process.

The second change is that lawyers have now got themselves into seats of power. Therefore, instead of drafting the wishes of the legislators and business drivers, they are in the front seat.

The third change is that of the increase in litigation.

The fourth change is that unelected officials whether in judicial or commissionary positions have decided it is OK to interpret the law according the their values and philosophies. It used to be a given that laws were interpreted according to the desires of the legislators at the time.

The academics have changed their thinking to " truth is a function of human consensus and cannot be measured by scientific measurements". That says that truth is what the activists yell the loudest. Say it often enough and it becomes the truth.

In science, you can have a rule of law for centuries and then one experiment proves it wrong and the theory must logically be debunked. However, with linguistic constructivism we have many, it appears to be the majority, of academics that believe that the truth comes from cultural interaction. This means that any theory can be found to be scientifically incorrect but remains fact because that is what we believe.

In science, you carry out an experiment and the results prove or disprove the hypothesis.

However, law is very much like constructivism. You have a precedent and no matter what the result of that precedent the law still demands that the law over rides common sense and logic.

The Law takes no account of whether t he precedent was successful or a miserable failure. It then puts the past directly into the future through the use of that precedent. Imagine if we did that in business or in our lives. Unfortunately, that is actually happening; because of the influence of the law in politics and business we are remaking the mistakes of the past over and over again. But that is only the half of it, the other half of the legal model is that once you have applied the precedent from the past you then have to apportion blame. There must be a number of parties and those parties must be blamed for what happened in the past. This apportionment of blame has infiltrated our social thinking. In the early days of Australian settlement there were fires, floods and wind. They destroyed our physical environment. We rebuilt and moved on. However, today we must have someone to blame. Was it the weather bureau, the flood gate operator, the electrical supply company, or the neighbour's tree. Something happened to my property and someone must be blamed and I must be recompensed. But worse than that we now must blame someone else for our own feelings. I was hurt, I was offended, I was oppressed. As a society, we do not take responsibility for ourselves, we look to the law to find blame and then we want recompense for the injuries inflicted.

The change from taking responsibility for ourselves to looking to our legal rights has changed our culture and our society.

As a nation, we do not look to the future, to build, to grow, to create. We, like the law, look to the past and look for someone to blame.

What follows is the most frightening observation. If you have been trained to think of precedent and apportionment of blame it is impossible to lead a corporate enterprise. It is the responsibility of the board to create a vison for the future. It is then the role of the lawyers to ensure that the future is within the law. The risk averse nature of a legal thought pattern is mutually exclusive with the thoughts required for a bright corporate future.

What follows is that legal minds are incapable of creating a future in a new world, and yet we have a parliament full of people trained to rule through precedent and apportionment of blame.

The Financial System

The Australian financial system is complex and made up of a number of financial entities such as individuals, households, businesses and governments who have a variety of needs such as spending, saving, borrowing and lending or investing. This all requires a huge number of transactions in a system that is heavily regulated by government. As a result, all these parties need a number of financial service providers to enable them to carry out their required transactions.

Financial System Basics

The basic function of the financial system is to allow people to buy and sell goods and services in an efficient manner. In short bartering didn't work. The total system is made up of people that carry out the transactions, provide services, provide the markets in which to trade, and regulate the industry.

You in the System

You have already gone to work and earned your pay packet. You come home with that money in cash or in your bank account from there you, normally carry out one of five different types of financial transaction.

Spend	We all know how to do that.
Borrow	If we want to buy something we do not have money for we can borrow more.
Insure	In life, there are many risks and you need to manage your risks. Some insurance is compulsory, eg, third party, other you make up your own mind, eg, health insurance.
Save	There are at least three things in your life you will have to save for. Your first house, educating your children and your retirement. All three are large expenditures that will need to be saved for over a long period of time.
Invest	Once you have saved money you will want to get the best return you possibly can.

Your financial needs

Spending	Access to cash, through an ATM. Credit cards, debit cards, blockchain transactions. How are you going to carry out your transactions?

Borrowing	How much do you need and when? You will need to understand the concept of risk and return. The higher your risk to a lender the higher the rate they will lend to you at.
Insurance	Your insurance needs are a function of your ability to take on risk.
Saving	To save well you need a plan, a budget and the willpower to follow through on the plan.
Investment	When you make an investment, you will strive to achieve a capital gain and an income. Your choice of investment will need to consider your time frame, your tax structure and your risk profile.

Financial Service Providers

These are the people and companies that provide your financial services. At some stage in your life you are likely to need the services of one of these service providers, just as at some stage you will need someone to service your car or provide hotel accommodation.

The financial service providers are:

The Reserve Bank. The role of the Reserve Bank of Australia (RBA) is set out in the *Reserve Bank Act 1959*. The bank conducts the country's monetary policy and issues its currency. It seeks to foster financial system stability and promotes the safety and efficiency of the payment system

The Banks. The role of a bank is to take in deposits from savers and make loans to borrowers. They derive an income from the rate differential. In the process, they also provide transactional services, physical storage and currency exchange. Modern banks have enhanced their product range to include anything from stockbroking to financial services. These are strictly not core banking activities.

Building Societies. They started the same as banks

collecting funds from savers and lending them to borrowers. They operate under a different set of rules to the banks.
- Credit Unions. Do almost the same things as Building Societies but started as Cooperative organisations.
- Investment Banks. Are essentially wholesale banks, as opposed to the retail banks.
- Finance Companies. Generally provide short-term finance, normally at higher interest rates.
- Superannuation Funds. All Australian employers must put 9.5% of the employee's wages into a superannuation fund that has the job of investing it on behalf of the employee for their use in retirement. There three types of Super Funds, Industry, Retail, and self managed.
- Fund Managers. Companies that pool funds from different sources and invest on behalf of the owners.
- Stock Brokers. Buy and Sell equities on the stock market on behalf of investors.
- Mortgage Lenders. They provide loans normally for the purpose of purchasing a home. They try to compete with banks by having lower overheads.
- Insurance Organisations. They provide either general or life insurance. They also branched out early in the last century into other investment services.

Why do you need to know all this? Mainly so you do not go to the wrong provider for a job. However, these days it is hard to know where some of the roles start and where they finish. As a young man, I was pretty naive and stupid. So when I needed money to buy a dining room table I set off to get a loan. I didn't know the difference between the organisations above. I went to my bank and asked for the loan. In those days, they did not get me to fill in 25 forms and then tell me that I was too high a risk. They just asked me a few questions and told me to go to another counter. Little did this little dummy know that I had just been moved from the Westpac Banking counter that provided loans at 6% to an AGC desk. This was the equivalent of moving from the palatial offices of Westpac in Collins Street to the back-alley loan sharks, only to me it looked like a 5 metre walk to another cubicle for a personal loan at an interest rate of 9%. I guess today you would just nimble it. The first of many times I got fleeced because I didn't know the system, the players and the roles. It can cost you a lot of money.

Financial Markets

All money flows through one of four markets. These markets are like any other markets. They could be the fish market or the flower market. They are a place were only that commodity is traded. The financial service providers above do their thing in the markets set out below.

Debt

All governments and companies need capital to work with. They get the capital by selling debt to the market. Just as with your finances there is short-term and long-term debt. The shortest form of debt is the short-term money market. This is where large amounts of money are put for very short periods even just overnight

Short-term debt comes in the form of bills, certificates of deposit, treasury notes, short-term securities.

Long-term debt comes in the form of Treasury bonds, semi-government bonds and corporate bonds. The debt market is really a capital market. Those with capital are lending it to those that want capital. The purchase of a bond gives you a capital return at the end of the period based on the market and a fixed-income during the period called a coupon.

Equity

Also known as the stock market or share market. This is the place you can buy a share in a company. In reply you get a share certificate and the opportunity to receive dividends. You invest in a company and you get the chance of a capital gain through the share price and the chance of an income through the dividend.

Foreign Exchange

The Forex market is where you change your Aussie dollars for the currency you need either where you going or where you want to buy something. The rate depends on the part of the total market you use. I used to have great discussions with fellow travellers about where the best place to change your money was. On reaching a new destination I used to go to the local ATM and take money out on AMEX. I always thought that was the best rate. But now, who knows? Make sure you do your homework.

Derivative Markets

I would classify derivatives as gambling not investing. It is a zero sum game market primarily operated by hedge funds through computers. If you think you can win against professionals and computers, be my guest.

Providers of Financial Advice

We have seen that the financial industry in Australia represents 12% of GDP. A significant part of that industry is the advisers who are all clambering to get you to pay them so they can show you what to do with your money. The list of advisers is long: financial planner, financial adviser, broker, stockbroker, accountants, solicitors, real estate agents, general insurance companies, life insurance companies, actuaries, banks, finance companies, building societies, fund managers. And all these want you to pay them for advice. The problem can be that you ask one for advice and they subcontract out part of the work to another part of the industry and suddenly your 10% return just dropped back to 6%.

The banks are being questioned at the moment. When I was working hard and not thinking properly about investments our bank manager asked us to attend a presentation. I suppose it was part ego, part fatigue, and part misguided trust that lead us to invest in a Financial Product via a bank. It was only when I read the fine print that I realised that the bank got a sales commission. The note was issued by The Financial Managers, who invested it in the Financial Managers Leverage Fund who invested in The Financial Managers Holdings who invested in the Financial Managers' Managers Fund who invested in a series of global funds who invested in actual companies. All in there were six levels of managers all taking fees along the way.

The Regulators

The world is full of social psychopaths and other people that have a different set of values to the majority. We have already seen that the government and policy makers are full of lawyers, and lawyers believe that you can regulate out bad behaviour. Centuries of precedent shows that is not true but those in government still believe it. The result is that we have the Australian Securities and Investment Commission (ASIC), the Australian Prudential Regulatory Authority (APRA) the RBA, the Australian Competition and Consumer Commission (ACCC) and the Australian Stock Exchange (ASX), all there to make sure we fill in a myriad of forms so that we will not get ripped off by a financial service provider. I ask, How is that working for us?

These regulate the industry using a number of acts of parliament including, the *Corporations Act 2001, Australian Securities and Investment Commission Act 2001, Anti–Money Laundering and Counter-Terrorism Financing Act 2006, Financial Transactions Reports Act 1988, Privacy Act 1988, Competition and Consumer Act 2010, National Consumer Credit Protection Act 2009*, and financial institutions' codes of practice, including the Electronic Funds Transfer Code of Practice.

Remember the biggest industry in Australia is the mining industry turning over $220 billion per year and the regulatory industry is in second place with $180 billion of cost to industry and government.

In economics, there is a law called the "Law of diminishing returns". It is used to refer to a point at which the level of profits or benefits gained is less than the amount of money or energy invested. That means, would you buy a $1,000 insurance policy to save $20? Probably not.

Australia, where are you?

We have spoken about the politics, economics and culture of our times. Here is an attempt to paint a picture of the environment in which we are living.

Government

Australia has moved from a centre governance position where a balance between left and right resulted in bi-partisan support for sensible and logical policies, to a centre left position where the left is never satisfied and good governance is overruled by politics.

The focus has moved from reform to political survival.

Identity politics has taken over from majority rule.

Our system has morphed from democracy to a form of bureaucracy. Let me be specific. Our laws are governed by bodies such as the UN, the EU, the IMF, the IPPC, all bodies run by unelected officials. Our courts are run by unelected officials who acknowledge that they interpret the law according to their values and philosophies and not according to the will of the elected legislature.

In addition to that we have a system where 60% of voters pay no net income tax, over 80% of retirees live on a full or part pension and over 25% of 18-24 year old rely on public money as their main source of income. In any normal democratic system there are the rules of conflict of interest. You do not get to vote at a body corporate meeting if you are not financial, you do not get to vote as a director if you have a conflict of interest, yet over half of the population is reliant on the government for their prime source of income and they get to vote on the government they want.

Our regulatory system has become the second largest industry in the country.

The twentieth century was a time of growth, personal freedom, and innovation. There is no doubt it was the greatest century in the history of homo sapiens. However in the last generation a strong pull to the left has resulted in the government controlling the education, health, prosperity, lifestyle and finances of individuals.

Some of you are saying that might be going a bit far. I suggest those people think a little deeper.

The government has changed the education system from one of didactic teaching to social experiential teaching.

Regarding health, governments control who gets what care, they control what research is carried out and what drugs are able to be taken.

Prosperity is controlled through taxation, regulation and public opinion. Both the government and the opposition openly tell us that anybody that has more than $1.6mill in super or a salary over $120,000 are filthy rich and deserves to be openly fleeced.

Lifestyle. The government spends millions telling people to slip, slop and slap, or life be in it. There are so many ways in which the government controls us. They are too numerous to mention. If you do not believe me then think of what happened on the Gold Coast in April 2018. The Gold Coast in Queensland hosted the Commonwealth Games. Months before the games were held the government started to tell people to go away, do not use the roads, avoid visiting the area. Schools were shut down, businesses closed for a week and whole residential buildings were vacated. The result was that there was no traffic congestion, businesses suffered because nobody came. The games were a financial disaster for the local business community who not only lost their business during the games period but also lost it for the Easter weekend before the games and the school holidays. Yes, the government controls our behaviour at every turn.

Finances. I see this as different to prosperity. Our government hates the rich, but it also wants to control the finances of the rest of the community. Anybody who pays attention will earn more in their lifetime from investment income than from earned income. The majority of this capital is in super funds and guess what they are controlled by the government. APRA, ACCC, FoFA, ASIC, FOS, CIO and the RBA. They h ave e nquiries i nto b anking, financial advice, derivatives, work practices and so on. All this results in further regulation which slowly takes away another degree of responsibility and freedom from you.

Before the twentieth century the majority of the world was ruled by authoritarian governments. During the twentieth century industrialisation produced democratic governments. However in the recent past democracy is retreating from the preferred governance system in the world. Not only are countries giving up on democracy those that remain are slowly given the democratic right of their constituents away. The advent of unelected legislative entities along with the transformation of the unelected judiciary into neo political institutions has resulted in a reduction of the powers of the elected legislature. In some democracies the majority of the voting public rely on the government for their principle source of income. The result is that in just over one century the world has gone from authoritarian government through the democratic phase and is now reverting to authoritarian governance. If you want to know how that works out research the Russian economy 1910-1950.

So the main thing you need to remember is that the government wants to control you. I should say it does control you.

In education through the curricula, the assessment system, programs such as safe schools, rules that control behaviour and much much more.

In housing through control of land releases, interest rates, taxation, infrastructure spending and regulation.

In health in everything from GP service delivery, think super clinics, to elective surgery and pharmaceuticals.

Sport has the AIS controlling our future athletes. Fisheries control where can fish. National parks controls where we can walk.

The government decides whether manufacturing industry survives or dies. It controls what movies we watch, what food we eat and what we can drink. You can't cut down a tree in your backyard or put up a shed to house your equipment without government control.

I watched the Hunger Games during the lead up to the recent election in Batman and realised that we are only a tiny step away from that sort of governance.

Economy

The processes of economic rationalisation and globalisation hand in hand with some very poor negotiations has resulted in Australia returning to its roots as a farm and a quarry.

Red and Green tape has reduced investment to decade low levels.

The main issue with the economy is that it is only mining, agriculture, manufacturing, international tourism and international education that creates wealth for the country. That is mining 12%, agriculture 10%, manufacturing 6%, tourism 0.2% and education 0.1% a total of 28.3% of the economy creates wealth. The government uses 36% to provide services, the construction industry uses 21% to provide accommodation and the finance industry spins 12% of the economy goes around in circles.

Australia's national debt position

Australia has record high levels of debt. Part of that debt is owed by the government and part by households. The problems are:

Government debt has been used for frivolous spending not infrastructure. That is the government has spent its debt on consumables and not on assets.

Household debt is primarily tied up in housing. Houses are not assets, they will not give you an income. Houses do not manufacture goods or create wealth.

A ratings downgrade means interest rates will go up increasing the spending on debt. At present both the government and households are spending significant amounts on financing debt. As interest rates rise, and they will, more money will be taken out of the economy to service the debt hence there will be less money available in the economy.

The money is going overseas. Both the banks and the government borrow money from overseas. The interest on the loans will be going offshore.

It will take a long time to fix. There are various ways to measure debt so let's be conservative. The government debt at present is about $800billion. Household and business debt is about $2.8trillion. Now the GDP of the economy is about $1.7trillion. Therefore as an economy of $1.7trill we need to pay off $3.6trill in debt. The government has agreed that there will be no budget surplus until at least 2021. That means the whole of the economy would have to work for 2 years to pay off the debt. On top of that there is interest to be paid. The bottom line is that the next generation are going to spend their entire working lives trying to pay off the debt created in the last decade. The Australian situation will be somewhere between where we are now and where Greece is now. The depth of the problem will be a function of when the country stops spending more than it earns.

How did we get here? Simple really, many politicians and economists convinced us that spending more than we earn was OK. The reality is that it all depends on what you spend it on. If a family borrows to go on holidays and buy consumables they get themselves into problems. However, if they borrow to buy appreciating assets then they can sell the assets at more than the borrowings and life moves on. Australia spent money on utes for people who did not need them, pink batts that later had to be pulled out, school halls that were expensive to build and have no balance sheet value, computers for school kids that have gone to the dump, expensive hospitals because of outrageous industrial-relations laws and building regulations, an expanded public service to give the money away.

Energy

In the past Australia had a major competitive advantage over most of the world: it had cheap energy. In Australia, we have abundant coal, gas and uranium; we should have had the cheapest electricity in the world.

I am not going to reiterate the technical aspects of the energy issues in the country. What I do want to do is to show you how debates can become complicated from a technical, financial, philosophical and ethical point of view.

The main sources of energy are coal, gas, hydro, wind, solar, storage(batteries), tidal, geothermal and nuclear. Each one of these has been debated in terms of cost, sustainability, environmental factors, social factors and governance factors. A huge matrix has been formed around which hardly anybody agrees.

A geologist would argue that carbon dioxide started in the atmosphere and then was transferred into vegetation through photosynthesis only to be buried and turned into coal, gas and oil. Therefore what is wrong with returning it to where it came from.

A technician would argue that the carbon cost of building, maintaining and disposing of wind generators is greater than the carbon credits created from reducing the burning of coal.

An economist would argue that a solar panel actually, without subsidies, costs $3.5/watt to install. On average it produces 4 watts per day or 1.46kW per year. Implies a return of 29.2cents per annum per watt at a sale price of 20cents per kWh. That is a return of 3.34% on capital after allowing for depreciation. Then of course at some stage, probably before the 20 years you are going to have to remove and dispose of the panels and the inverter at what cost?

An ethically minded person would say they really do want to get solar, why should the rest of the community pay me subsidies to provide cheap power at their cost. A perfectly rational person would argue that tidal energy is a known dependable source and why are we not focusing on taming the tides. An engineer would tell you that small compact nuclear power stations are not only safe but can be sited near the consumers therefore reducing transmission requirements and losses.

No matter what anybody tells you there is no answer that will satisfy everybody's needs. Somebody is going to hate each one of the perspectives above. What you need to understand is that Social Justice Warriors (SJW's) will linquistically contruct truths that are an intersubjective consensus amongst people of their beliefs and those truths will have no relation to any objective measurements or process.

Rent-seeking

Rent-seeking is defined as the practice of manipulating public policy or economic conditions as a strategy for increasing profits.

Rent-seeking behaviour is defined as the use of resources of a company, an organisation or an individual to obtain economic gain from others without reciprocating any benefits to society through wealth creation.

To get your head around the concept of rent-seeking you need to pull together everything we have been through to date: politics, economics, and culture.

In politics, we have a socialist government that wants to control production and distribution of goods and services. They do this by making their preferred products more attractive to the market by either subsidising them or giving them grants to make their production more profitable. So a rent-seeker is someone who goes along to government and lobbies them into believing that their product is good for society. When the government gets on board it subsidises the product and in turn manipulates the free market.

Major rent-seekers in Australia have been the renewables industry. The government pays them to produce power that is more expensive for the consumer.

There has been worldwide discussion over whether some of these projects are positive for the community in the long-term. The point is that government subsidies are market manipulation and contrary to the values of a free market.

The Mindset of Australians

Four significant changes have occurred over the last century.

Self-reliance has moved to entitlement

In the early 20th century, there were retirees that had fought in world wars and been through depressions—there was one in the 1890s and another in the 1930s—and saved enough to look after themselves in retirement. In the 1920s, over 80% of people over 65 years of age were self-funded retirees. The most important issue is that they were proud of it. They would stand in public places and tell everybody that they could look after themselves. One hundred years later, over 80% of those aged over 65 are on some kind of government pension. The scary thing is that they are proud of it. You hear people talking how they have given their money away to their children, or buried it in their principal place of residence allowing them to claim on the public purse. A number of years ago I was talking with a person who was traveling around in a caravan. They said the major discussion in the caravan parks was how to get money out of the government. In 2015, the government had 20 major welfare programs (including 55 sub-categories) costing $152 billion, which goes to $187 billion in four years. This is basically the total income tax take. So we collect income tax to redistribute wealth, and at the same time nothing gets done. That is unsustainable. Looking at the 2016 Budget Update there are 17 categories reviewed in relation to tax and benefits, of those 11 receive more in handouts than they pay in tax. There was a famous Kennedy quote. "Ask not what your country can do for you, but ask what you can do for your country". In Australia, we have well and truly crossed the line. With 10% of the working population paying 50% of the income tax and 20% paying nearly 80% of the income tax that supports over 60% of the population, we now officially have a socialist society where it is better and easier to live off government benefits than it is to take a risk. Again, that is unsustainable, as was found in southern Europe. You as an individual need to ask yourself where you want to be. In the end, you end up on a pension of $23,000 per year or you fund yourself to a better lifestyle. If you start at 20 years of age and put $100 per month into a super fund you will retire on $750,000. If you work for the same period on the average wage and put in 9.5% super guarantee you will have a balance of $5.2m at age 65. It's not too difficult to break the entitlement cycle. It just needs a plan and a bit of self-control.

Emphasis has moved from responsibilities to rights

In the days when Europeans settled Australia there were no rights just responsibilities. You were responsible for your own life, be it your health, your welfare or that of your future.

The Commonwealth of Australia was formed in January 1901 and a history of pensions and benefits was born. These government handouts took responsibility from the needy. As time went on there was a slow change to the definition of needy and a progressively larger group received government benefits.

With the addition of benefits came the slow erosion of responsibilities. As the body of legislation grew so did responsibilities diminish. Then came the beginnings of the nanny state. Legislation was enacted that required people to behave in certain ways. Suddenly, we were not making decisions for ourselves, those decisions were being made for us. Legislation slowly removed responsibilities and increased the rights of individuals.

The result is a legal environment where the individual can make a choice as to whether they use the system to maximise their rights or take responsibility for themselves. Obviously, this is an area that creates much discussion and strong feelings.

Let's rewind to the days of Federation, when free men were given parcels of land to farm. They lived with their families in the bush with no infrastructure, no medical care and no government back up. These families had to take full responsibilities for themselves. If a child got sick, did they travel for a day or two for medical attention or did they stay put and hope the crisis passed. If the house was burnt down or flooded out, they rebuilt there was no one to blame.

Now wind forward to 2015 where people fall in front of cars, into swimming pools and blame the owners. Blame the doctor if the child doesn't get better or the electrician if the house burns down.

As individuals, we have to make up our mind: are we going to take responsibility for ourselves or are we going to rely on government handouts, legal arguments and our rights? If, as a society, we all want to blame others, we need to think about where that is going to lead us and the society.

Saving for a rainy day has moved to spend it now there will be plenty later

Let's just have another little history lesson. Bankcard was the first credit card that came to Australia, in 1974. That is only 43 years ago, before that there was no credit for the average person. Your wage came in a little pay packet with notes and coin. You took the money home and used it according to your budget. So much for rent, food, health and so on. If you did not have the folding stuff in your pocket you could not spend it. There was no thought of spending without having the cash in your pocket.

Most people set out a budget and when they got their pay packet they would run down to the bank and put the amount assigned for saving in a savings account. You didn't have money in your pocket so you couldn't spend it. Then the credit card came along and people started to spend it before they earned it.

The result has been people cannot pay their credit card bills on time and are therefore paying up to 20% interest on the credit they have borrowed from the bank. When this goes too far they then have to nimble it, a forced savings plan at a very high interest rate.

There used to be a book we read at school called The Bible; it had lots of really good stories in it. One of the stories was about seven good years and seven hard years. Guess what, that is what happens in life. Ask your parents, grandparents or anybody that has been around long enough and they will tell you "it never rains it pours". When things are good it seems like you can do no wrong, and when things go badly it appears that absolutely nothing will go right for you. There will be seven good years when you have a great job, earn lots of money and remain in good health, and nothing goes wrong with the car or the house. After those seven good years, things will happen. The car will break down, the house will get flooded, you will lose your job and your partner will get sick. The point being that you need to save like hell in the seven good years so that when the seven bad years come along you can ride over the hump.

Parenting has moved from strict to lenient, and from mentor to friend

The job of a child is to test the boundaries. The job of the parent is to show the child where those boundaries are. Well that seems to have changed along the way. Parents want to be friends with their children.

We need to go back to the basic rules of life. When you work on the factory floor you can drink with the boys in the bar, but as soon as you join the management you must drink in another bar. They say one of the loneliest jobs in the world is that of a sea captain. It is just not possible to maintain discipline and fraternise with the crew.

As a parent, I have no problem traveling business class while the kids are in the rear of the plane. Once you let them up front they are there for good alongside you as an equal. Then when you want to explain where the boundaries are your power has been eroded.

Numerous friends have confided to me that they have spoiled their children, and now they are paying for it. A child can become a friend when they share equally in the responsibilities. They pull their weight around the house and behave on your level. This is simply not likely to happen. So if you want to do the right thing by your children, you had better keep in mind at all times that you are showing them where the boundaries are. When they first learn to walk, you explain it is not a good idea to walk on the road. During adolescence, you need to explain that an adult takes responsibility not only for themselves but also for others in the pack. Because I am perceived as too tough, I do not consider graduating or getting a job a great achievement. It is something that is expected if you want to join the human race. However, the day your child takes you out to dinner, that is a day on which you can be really proud.

A parent needs to mentor their children. That is, they need to be an experienced and trusted adviser. As opposed to a friend that has a bond of mutual affection. It is your decision: do you want to have mutual affection with your children, or do you want to have their trust and advise them on how to get through the ravages of life?

In years gone by children left home at 16 to 18, they were still adolescents, not yet fully adults and were therefore treated as children until the day they left home. Now we have children hanging around the home until they are 30 and more. During those times if they are befriended they do not get the advice they need to grow into full adulthood. Hence, we have a lot of friendly relationships and 30-year-olds who are whingeing about the fact that they cannot buy a house.

And the four of these are all told in one story

In the 1960s Italian and Greek migrants came to Australia. They moved from their homelands because there were no opportunities there, and moved to the land of opportunity. They worked hard and they saved. They were in the main uneducated but looking to build a future. They came at a time when Australians were resourceful, machines were fixed with fencing wire or anything to hand. Innovation came out of necessity. And while they lacked in education they saw that for their children to grow the children needed to have a good education.

Those children were brought up in a strict family atmosphere. They worked in the family business after school, on the weekend and all through the school holidays. They were never paid and were told that they were contributing to the family. The family was generally three generations under one roof. The grandparents cooked, cleaned and minded the young children. The parents worked long hard hours. Parties were restricted to weddings, anniversaries, religious holidays and the big birthdays.

The biggest birthday was at 18. That was pay day for the children. After working a lifetime in the family business, they got their first pay. That came in the form of a car. The louder, the flashier and the faster the better. This went on for a generation until two things happened. The kids, now more highly educated, started to reject the strict family work life. They convinced their parents that they could not study and work at the same time. The parents continued to work hard, but the kids backed off.

The parents did not know or see what was happening. They assumed the kids were doing the right thing as they did, but they did not understand the needs of the education system and were therefore hoodwinked into giving the kids an easy ride. It was easy to spend hours in your room doing stuff and convincing your parents you were working. The thought that they were entitled to an easy ride was being planted.

The other thing that happened was that the older Australians saw these immigrants buying their kids flash cars. They thought it was a show of how well the parents were doing, and jealousy set in. We cannot have these poor immigrants buying GTHOs for their kids.

So the age of buying cars for the kids began. It was the establishment keeping up with the immigrants gone crazy. Suddenly you had a whole generation of 20-year-olds that had never done a day's work in their lives being given cars on their 18th birthday. The age of entitlement was borne.

From there it only got worse. Working through university became the gap year. Hard-fought apprenticeships became university degrees. Article clerks became overpaid researchers. From the 1960s, where the average child started work in their teens, worked through school and university, we now have 25-year-olds that have made their way through school, the gap year and university without ever having a job.

The same thing happened in the boardrooms around Australia. The older board members did not understand the new technology and therefore they outsource their IT services to young people who had no idea. From that point on the board lost control of the business. When once the board was full of people that knew how to run the business, suddenly it was full of lawyers, bankers, and other specialists that knew something of corporate maneuvers but little of the actual business they were in.

The Integration of Immigrants

The culture in Australia today has been moulded from clay made from a little piece of many cultures from lands all over the world. The driving force of all the cultures that came to this continent was one of survival. It is hard in the 21st century to imagine that 100 years ago 85% of the world's population were in poverty, and at the time of the first fleet more than 95% of the world's population lived in poverty and nearly 90% lived in extreme poverty. It was therefore imperative that every culture had survival as its main driving force.

There are many still coming to Australia for a better life, however as a society we are making it harder and harder for these people to become integrated into the Australian community.

Language has always been a major issue and that used to get solved through the workplace. However now we have removed most of the jobs that do not require language therefore these people are now forced to stay at home on social welfare until the next generation comes along. The result is that communities of non-English-speaking people build up where they are unable to exchange cultures with the surrounding community.

Summary

In politics, there is the left wing and the right wing. The left wing believes that everyone should be equal, and the right wing believes that there are natural inequalities, and these should be fostered and not destroyed. In finance, there is capitalism versus socialism. The capitalist believes in market forces and individual ownership. The socialist believes in markets controlled by the state and state ownership. In culture, there are the conservatives who range from those that do not want change without a good reason to those that want to go back to the past. And the progressives who want to use advancements in science, technology, economics and social organisation to improve the human condition.

Let's just remember that during the last 100 years world poverty has been reduced from 85% to 8.4% of the population. Not a bad result from a dysfunctional democratic capitalist system.

Australia, where will you be in 2065?

The left are moving towards equality. That means that the whole population, less the elites, will be reduced to the lowest common denominator. It is possible this will result in biological changes between the elites and the useless. The other option is that the useless class will be kept happy with drugs and video games while existing on a Universal wage.

We can see that the picture we have in the world at the moment is not looking good in a political, economic and culture sense.

It is virtually a fait accompli that democracy as a global governance system does not and will not work.

Financially, ethically, and morally it has been proved conclusively that communism and socialism do not work. True capitalism has yet to be tried, but in the political climate is never likely to be tried.

Religion has been driven into the background and linguistic constructivism has taken its place. This has left a huge hole in the cultural development of the world, one that is yet to be filled.

Accepting the fact that socialism cannot continue on an international basis, democracy cannot continue on an international basis and the basic values of all cultures are being questioned, then where are we going?

Yuval Noah Harari is a voice of change at present. Read Homo Deus or, for the lazy ones, watch him at TED Talks. His hypothesis is that humans started thousands of years ago when they gained the ability to live in groups larger than 150 people. They have now outgrown the ability to be governed nationally and the biggest problem we face is globalism versus nationalism. Harari maintains that all the problems of the next 50 years require global solutions and that national solutions will only add to the overall problem.

Hypothesis is defined as "a supposition or proposed solution made on the basis of limited evidence as a starting point for further investigation." That is the great point of his work. He does not say he has the answers he only proposes the questions and asks us to use his work as a starting point for further discussion and debate. This is a very different approach to the activists that think they know the answers and are not prepared to listen to any discussion or debate.

Harari starts with the premise that AI will leave most the world without a job. In the not too distant future, the vast majority of people will rely on a basic income from the government. The questions are who the government will be and what is considered basic. His next premise is that all solutions will be global, yet at the same time he has no idea what the governance system looks like in the future.

While Harari believes we cannot go back, we have to move forward, I would argue that to make good long-term progress you often have to take two steps forward and one step back.

The last 72 years the world has taken a number of steps forward trying to develop global governance. By no stretch of the imagination could you say these were going well, in fact even if you look at other world bodies such as the International Olympic Committee (IOC) and FIFA, we can see that the world has issues in playing nicely. There are national interests, personal interests and crime that have to be considered. So while Harari says we need to learn how to play together, he makes no reference as to how that is going to happen. I would argue that we need to take a step back and look at what has happened and try it again rather than taking a broken model and trying to move forward with it.

Changes in the last 50 years

You will be retiring in 2067, so what has happened in the last 50 years.

Let's go back to 1967. Television was around with only three channels and in black and white.

Telephones had yet to have subscriber trunk dialling (STD); long-distance calls were placed through an operator. There were no mobile phones, and there was no internet and no video.

Automatic cars had just been released on the market and safety belts were optional. There were no credit cards, when traveling you took travellers' cheques. You needed a different currency for each country in Europe and there was immigration between countries. However, there were no security checks at airports.

You could do what you liked on your property, there were no helmets for bikes or motorbikes. It was legal to urinate on the rear driver's side tyre, and there were no speed limits in country areas. Pubs closed at 6.00pm and no shops were open on the weekends.

Australia's major income earner was wool and manufacturing employed the bulk of the workforce.

Employment

It is well recognised that artificial intelligence will be taking over a lot of jobs. Australia has lost hundreds of thousands of manufacturing jobs, call centres have gone overseas. It is likely that some of your accounting work or legal work is being done overseas, but that is only the tip of the iceberg.

At present, there are thousands of managed funds and financial advisers. I would suggest that in a few years funds will be run by computers and to get financial advice you will fill in an online form and the computer will tell you what to do.

While in the last 50 years we have gone from households with one person employed to households with two people employed, it is likely that in the next 50 years we will go back to only the one employed if that.

You can look at it from two perspectives. The first is that the change to employment structures is just not fair and that as a result you are looking forward to a global government giving you a universal wage in order to survive. The second is that there are going to be so many opportunities out there. It is going to be difficult to pick those to have a go at.

Income

Competition for wages increasing. Your competitors are the young and well educated from Asia that are on the end of any internet connection and the growing field of artificial intelligence. Between these two there is going to be increased downward pressure on wages. The era of growing wealth through high incomes is at an end. When you think of it capital was king from the dawn of time until the industrial revolution. It has only been in the last century that income has been able to create wealth.

Income will be replaced by capital has the driving force behind wealth creation in the middle classes.

Governance

Global governance has a long way to go. Think of the issues in Australia. Do we remain in the Commonwealth, do we remain a monarchy or do we become an independent republic? Given that the main thing holding us up in becoming a republic is an agreed role and system of voting for the head of state, it would appear that a change to our governance system is a fair way off. Now translate that into a global scenario. We certainly hope that the world will not need two world wars and a decade long recession to figure out a solution, however with differences in politics, finances and cultures, it would appear that global governance is a pipe dream at present.

Culture

The great big melting pot sounds great in theory and exciting when put to music, however in reality it is a very different thing. Later in the manual we will talk about the need to have a goal or a vision when you start a project. The hardest part of the cultural melting pot is to put together a vision for the cultural integration of the world. One global culture, in a world where the UN cannot agree that the Syrian president killing a few hundred thousand people is not such a good idea and that something needs to be done about it.

Vision for the Future

On a recent trip to the US I found myself walking across the Golden Gate Bridge faced by a horde of cyclists coming towards me. I looked over the 1.2 metre high rail to the left and noticed there was nothing stopping me vaulting over the rail and plunging into the water 400 ft below. I then looked back to the cyclists with half of them not wearing helmets. Never in Australia. I know the regulatory march started in the US but they still have freedoms that we can only dream of in Australia.

That night we were out to dinner, and as the elderly do, I went off to the bathroom. The door from the restaurant opened directly into the washroom and from there to the cubicles where the doors opened inwards. A light went on in this old mind.

I remember when the conservation movement took hold of councils around Australia in the area of waste water quality. When putting new standards into place the councils would collect all the standards, already in place, from all around the country. They would then make their new standards the same or higher than those already existing. That way the council made sure they could not be litigated against for not having tough enough standards.

How about we reverse that process. How about we go around the world and look at all the regulations in place and bring ours back to those that have been working for years instead of making them tougher, make them workable.

Many would argue that 1700 people have jumped off the Golden Gate Bridge. Others would argue that they hurt nobody in doing that, however suicide by single vehicle accident potentially harms many.

Conclusion to Defining Your Environment

This book is about you planning your life. For you to plan it we are looking at the physical, political, economic, financial and cultural environment in which you live. After defining your environment, you are going to define you as an individual. Your strengths and weaknesses. You will then develop a vision of where you want to take yourself within your environment. Once the vision is set you will develop a plan to attain that vision. This is the same process that businesses should use. They define their environment. Work out their strategic competitive advantages and then create a mission and a vision. They define production, financial, marketing plans and put in place a risk-management safety net.

That is a logical process where you take the past and then infuse it into the future, with a focus on using your strengths and allowing for your weaknesses.

We have learned

The key component to defining our political, financial and cultural environment is the speed of change.

It took 600,000 years to go from the control of fire to the control of electricity, and then only another 70 years from electricity to nuclear power. A thousand years from the first coins to the first credit card and then only 50 years to paywave and bitcoin. While people have been travelling the world for thousands of years it wasn't until 50 years ago air travel was commercialised. The WWW was born in 1990, that is only 28 years ago and now we cannot live without it.

In the year 1900 over 85% of the world's population lived in poverty. All but a few spent all their waking life trying to survive and feed their families. The human DNA is geared towards procreation and survival, yet 100 years later in Australia "only the top 20% of households pay net tax. The bottom 6.9million households, while often incurring income tax liabilities and regularly paying GST, received more in cash welfare and services than they paid in."

Today 8.4% of the world's population live in poverty, therefore within 100 years the role of the majority of humans has changed from procreation and survival to being supported by a benevolent government. The question here becomes how can the human psychology make the jump from survival to nurturing. We see the answer to that question in the number of people that need therapy, intervention and rehabilitation. It is a known fact that human satisfaction begins just outside your comfort zone, yet we are living in a world that goes to great lengths to ensure you do not have to step outside your personal comfort zone. The ultimate form or torture is to have to live in an environment with sensory deprivation. Living with the thousands of negative thoughts you bombard yourself with every day and no external input to drown out the pain. Next on the list must be a life where you are never challenged, never put outside your comfort zone and never learn to deal with the pain of getting over the oppressions that naturally come with life.

The left's answer to the new environment is a universal wage where you will never be pushed, you will never be in pain and you will always be protected by society. The right's answer is for each and every one of us to take responsibility for themselves. We are hard wired to carry a load. If we do not pick up a load we lose the meaning of life and that can only lead to pain and suffering.

Your job is to study your environment, feel it, understand it and become part of it. Learning about your environment is paramount to developing a fulfilling worthwhile life.

Why do I have to do this, my parents never did?

The answer is the speed of change. My generation was given a life expectancy of 65 years. We left school at 17, 4 years training and into the workforce at 21. You were expected to work until 60 and then have 5 years in retirement. That life did not require a plan. You swam with the tide. Now you are educated until 24, you burn out at 45, reinvent yourself as a consultant until 65, retire and become a mentor until 75, then you get to retire. In the meantime you will need to buy a house by the time you are 35 which will be 7 to 10 times your salary. You will need to educate your children between 40 and 55. And then you will need to have saved enough in super by 68 in order to live out your expectations in retirement. Hopefully you will also put in place an intergenerational wealth creation process for the benefit of future generations. That requires a plan.

3
Balance

Life is all about balance. It is a balance of five factors: lifestyle, job satisfaction, financial rewards, kudos and morals/ethics.

Most achievers want to fit huge amounts into their lives and often forget to balance them out.

Strategy comes down to a balance between aggression and defence.

Your investment portfolio will need to be balanced between capital growth and income, between high and low risk. It needs to be balanced between local and International and between industrial market sectors. In short, life is one big balancing act.

So let's get a look at the five factors you are going to use to balance your lives.

Kudos

Wanting to be liked. Seeking acclaim or praise for exceptional achievement.

Kudos is a function of your environment and your own personality. I lived in an environment where kudos was rarely given, but there again it wasn't expected.

Move forward a couple of generations and if you do not tell your staff how great they are on a weekly or even daily basis they will think they are being disrespected. So the amount of kudos craved for and given is very much a sign of the times.

At the same time, some people need more kudos than others.

There are a couple of things you need to get clear in your head.

Do I need respect from somebody else because I do not respect myself?

If you set yourself clear quantified targets you will find you need less kudos from others as you meet the targets.

Lifestyle

How you spend your time, work, family, sports, the arts, holidays. There are just so many hours in the day and yes, we all need rest and relaxation. How are you going to spend your time? Lifestyle has changed so much in the last century. In the 1930s, most people spent most of their time just surviving. Even during the period of the 1950s to 1960s people would buy a house that had no carpet, no soft furnishing and no landscaping. As a result, they would spend the next decade finishing their house. Until 1988 and expo in Brisbane, dining out was a once a year event. There are 168 hours in a week, how are you going to spend them. Later we will be working on financial budgets but for the moment we need to work on time budgets. You have 168 hours in a week and 8,760 hours in a year. How are you going to use your hours?

Lifestyle is a function of your, geographical location place of work, where your home is, your working hours, family, friends, health, fitness, sleep, recreation and hobbies.

Job Satisfaction

Some people live to work and others work to live.

There is a quote that says "Every job is the same after 6 months." and that from a jet fighter pilot. Most jobs are repetitive so you have better like doing the repetitive stuff.

I would seriously suggest that if you want to take some time out use it to work in the job environment of your chosen career. It is painful to see people that have spent 4 years training for a job to realise after a year or two that the job environment is not for them.

Job Satisfaction is a function of your place of work, corporate size, proximity to others, proximity to infrastructure, noise, temperature, working hours, and more. Do not just focus on your perception of the job.

Financial reward

For a happy and contented life, learn to make your own decisions and wait until you really want something. Always remember being wealthy is earning one more dollar a year than you spend.

My belief is that it comes down to embracing hunger. Sometimes you just have to have that new phone, laptop, car or holiday. Many people today buy clothes they never wear, new devices they do not need and holidays they cannot afford.

You have to pick a career that will give you what you need financially but balances with your lifestyle and job satisfaction. To get the equation right, you will need to define your financial requirements and then get the job that gives you the best balance.

Morality/Ethics

Judeo-Christian values are being superseded by legislation and regulation. The courts have taken over from the Church in monitoring our values.

Ethics and morals

Morals are how you treat people you know. Ethics are how you treat people you don't know. Your morality is what makes you a good wife or husband, dad or mother. A good daughter or son. A good friend. Even a good employee or boss to the people you know personally in the company. Your ethics are what makes you a good politician. It is what makes you a statesman. It is also what makes you a good, humane CEO of any large company (and yes, you can make money and pay your employees well.).

Social Psychopaths

It has been well documented that about 10% of the population have some sort of social psychopathy. Key traits that sociopaths and psychopaths have in common, include: A disregard for laws and social mores. A disregard for the rights of others. A failure to feel remorse or guilt. A tendency to display violent behaviour.

The big question is how to deal with social psychopaths. Because they feel no remorse or guilt there is no way you can negotiate with them. The only way to deal with them is to remove yourself from the relationship. This can be incredibly hard at times, but you need to be cognisant of your situation.

When you get the balance wrong

There are plenty of cases where people get the balance wrong.

It is very common for an incorrect balance to fall apart in middle age. A family is full of energy when they first get married, they buy the house and then do the renovation adding the bill onto the mortgage. They then send the kids to private schools and borrow the money so they can keep living the grand lifestyle. The bigger the salary the bigger the mortgage and loan because they think the money is going to come in forever.

About the time they turn 55, they realise they are tired of their job, the kids are leaving school and they are left with this great big debt. They calculate how long it will take to work the debt off and freak out when they realise that they will have to work at their now boring job until they are 70 before they can retire. Bad balance.

4
Fifty-Two Things I have Learned

This chapter is a list of some of the things I have learned along the way. They fit into many different sections.

1. Teamwork

To achieve really great things, it needs a team. In sport you need a coach, attacking players, defensive players and someone to organise it all. In business you need a visionary, an administrator and a technician. On the stage you need the producer, director, leads and chorus. A band does not function without a team. Even Ed Sheeran needs a manager and roadies. For the team to be successful, each of the elements needs to be in equal abundance. If the defence, the administrator or the artist rules then the others lose interest and the synergy is lost. Great achievements, and great achievers, require a team.

2. Vision

The old adage of the rudderless ship is so true. If you want to go somewhere you need to know where you are going and map out the route. You also need to know when you want to get there. Pretty simple, I need to be at school at 8.30am. I need to finish my report by Thursday afternoon. The bigger the project the harder it is to define and measure. My children need to be able to support themselves by the time they are 21? My business needs to turn over $3m in the 2020–21 financial year? I want to be able to retire with an income of $200,000 when I am 60? To publish four articles in a professional magazine by Christmas 2020.

The vision needs to have two elements. The first is a quantity. The second element is a time frame.

Organisations went through a stage of "motherhood statements". Our vision is to be the best service provider in our class. What does that mean?

If you want to go somewhere you need to quantify it and then put a timeframe on. That is sometimes the hardest part of the project.

3. Measurement

It you want something to get better, measure it. Human nature is a funny thing. Even with slothful individuals it is in our nature to want to achieve more and therefore if you measure something people will automatically try to make it better. Runners in the morning naturally want to measure their performance and better their times.

The difficult part is getting the right measure.

4. Authority

People generally, and children in particular, love authority. There has been much discussion about the new generations not being tolerant of authority. I believe the issue today is that there is no authority. Teachers are not allowed to discipline children; the rules do not allow it. Employers cannot sack employees; Fair Work will not let them. Even the prime minister cannot carry out his plan; the senate will not let him. And of course, parents are not consistent in their message. Therefore, the children do not know how to recognise authority. Once upon a time there was the authority in a title, not today. However, my experience is that given real authority children respond very well. The problem is how to exert authority. It is not that the receivers are not hearing the message.

5. Learn to embrace hunger

We humans can never get enough of a good thing, whether it is physical, emotional or spiritual, we always want more. History shows that those that get it together learn to embrace the feeling of hunger. Meditation and fasting reset your needs. Without a reset you just eat more and more.

I had not eaten tomato sauce for years, but when the grandkids came 18 months ago I bought some tomato sauce for them. When putting some on my snags, I thought it tasted sweet. On reviewing the label, I found the tomato sauce was 30% sugar, and the BBQ sauce was 50% sugar. I was then told the reason McDonald's put the pickles in the Big Mac was that without it the Big Mac would be classified as confectionery and not a snack food.

We like the taste of sugar and fat, and the purveyors of food have slowly built up the percentage of fat and sugar in all foods. Unless you go back to basics, your taste buds will continually crave more.

Once upon a time going to the movies once a month was a treat. Then it became once a week, now we have the new trend of people watching a whole season of a TV show in one sitting.

They used to televise one football match a week with highlights from the others. Now we get all matches live and then replays two and three times. Married couples used to start in a single-room apartment and work their way up to a three-bedroom house. Now they start with the three-bedroom house and work their way up to… One car used to be enough, now we need two or three.

Whether it be religion, sex, food, movies, toys or exercise. We all get a hit out of each of them and then become evangelists, sex maniacs, gluttons, collectors or gym junkies.

The only way to break the cycle is to embrace hunger. Recognise, unlike the frog, that the water is heating up and back off. Go without and reset the baseline. If you do not, the baseline will increase until you reach the absurd.

6. H=R/E: Happiness equals reality divided by expectations

If you have high expectations, your happiness level is reduced and you become a grumpy old man. If you have low expectations the reality will exceed your expectations resulting in a high happiness level. Of course, if your expectations are too low then you get a fake high. Balancing your expectations with reality is one of the most important skills to learn. It always has been and always will be a question of balance.

7. The information world has swamped the thinking world

Only 20 years ago the hardest thing about making a decision was getting enough information. Today the biggest issue is sifting through the information and weeding out the relevant facts. In schools and university, we teach facts and processes. The art of thinking is no longer taught. It is becoming harder and harder to think laterally because we are forced down the narrow tracks created through legislation and regulations. When asked, Einstein stated that he would never have created his work had he had a formal education. The narrow focus has increased dramatically since his day. When was the last time you put yourself in a vacuum and just thought through an issue?

There is so much information you have to figure out which is real and which information is linguistically constructed.

8. There are two things to which people completely close down: Retirement and aged care

Retirement. People under the age of 55 just do not want to know about retirement. Having said that, retirement is an old-fashioned word, it is really now a change of career path. They think their youth energy levels and their earning capacity will go on forever. As soon as you mention Superannuation or investment skills they run a mile. I have friends, especially those in professions that will have to work until they are 75 just to pay off the school fees, the mortgage and the personal loans. Start to discuss investment plans and lifestyle changes and they change the subject immediately.

Aged Care. As with retirement even highly intelligent people turn off as soon as you mention residential aged care. I have friends with parents in their 90s that will not even discuss the subject.

9. We have become risk averse

I was speaking with a teacher recently. She was telling me that the greatest change in her environment was the lack of band aids. In primary school 40 years ago, nearly every kid had grazes, bruises and scratches. At any one time, there was a kid in the class with a plaster cast helping heal a broken bone. Now the band aid is the exception. In the last decade, the number of new business applications has dropped by over 30%. As a society, we are told that everything out there is dangerous and we should be afraid. Regulations have driven risk underground to the point that people are just not trying. The corporate structure is such that small players do not even get a chance to quote. The economy used to be driven by enthusiastic young entrepreneurs, now we are driven by government and corporate bureaucrats that would not understand "having a go" if they fell over it. We have changed from "she'll be right mate" to "It's all too hard." And the scary thing is that the vast majority thinks that is a good thing.

10. The 80–20 principle, teams

I have called this "The 80–20 principle, teams" because the 80–20 is so true in many parts of life, but today I wanted to focus on teams.

In any team, there will be 20% overachievers, 70% workhorses and 10% that just will not cut it. There have been a number of managers that fire 10% of their workforce every year just to obey this law.

I found it hard to believe that 80% of people simply did not want to achieve. In 1920, 20% of people over the age of 65 were on the pension. Today 80% of people over 65 are on the pension. Only 20% of retirees are self-funded. The rule applies. So the aim is to inspire the 20%, nurture the 70%, and bring the 10% under control. Fact—10% of the population is at one level or another, a social psychopath.

11. The 2,2,½ rule is now the 4,4,¼ rule

I was first told of the 2,2,½ rule when I was 19. He was a fine Jewish gent. He was still loading the dye drums at 70 when his foreman was not at work. Very hands on. Very Jewish. Personalised number plates came to Victoria in about 1970. He signed up and got JEW 000 immediately. We were talking about a project and he told me never forget the 2,2,½ rule. I said what's that, Don? He said whatever it is you are going to do it will take twice as long, cost twice as much and be half as effective as you first thought. At 19, I had no idea what he was talking about. Now I think it has moved onto the 4,4,¼ rule. The extra costs of regulation today have been superimposed on the natural blow out of wishful thinking. And the fact that nobody can make a decision has meant that time frames are blown out of all perspective.

12. Gold nuggets take patience to find

When I was traveling before the days of iPads I used to buy books and read them on planes and in hotel rooms. A lot of these books were business and self-help books. Some were classics such as *The 7 Habits of Highly Successful People* and *The Psychology of Winning*. Others just made a point. Often that point was a single sentence or a paragraph. You had to read the whole book to find the one little sentence of worth. The same applied to seminars and courses. It is worth wasting the time and going through the boredom to find that one little nugget.

13. 10% of the population are classified as social psychopaths

I have run into numerous people in my life that appear to act without any thought for others. In some recent experiences, someone classified a person to me as being a social psychopath. So I looked it up and started doing some research. It appears a social psychopath has no conscience, is narcissistic, and plays the game of self-gratification at another person's expense. They have no feelings but study others and learn to show the feelings they wish to, making them chameleon-like. They are charming and cut a wide swathe through society, leaving a wake of ruined lives behind them.

The scary thing is that in this research I found that 10% of the population could be affected in one way or another by this affliction. What you have to remember with these people is that you cannot reach them because they have no emotions and therefore no guilt. It explains the level of bullying that we find in schools and in the workplace.

Prof Robert Hare has spent over 25 years researching psychopaths yet he stated recently that he had a lab manager with the affliction. Because he had not spent enough time with her he missed all the signals. In some ways, it makes it easier to understand some people's behaviour.

14. Real power is hidden

When dealing with the Chinese you sit at a table with 8–10 people. You are never told who holds the real power. In Australia, the average super fund run by the unions or the finance sector has returned 7.4% over the last ten years. The actual return of the funds is 11.4% before fees and charges. There is now about $2.5 trillion in super funds. The union controlled funds, or industry funds, control about $1 trillion. That means they have an income of $40 billion per year. Once they take out costs and salaries to old union employees they are left with over $15 billion in income. That income was used to put Labor governments in power in Victoria and Queensland. It is only because they went too far in NSW that Baird managed to survive. Mick Kelty took Paul Keating's gift and developed an income stream which means the unions do not need members. Andrews immediately put the CFMEU back on worksites, and now Palaszczuk is using state funds to take a "positive, supportive role" in the recruitment by unions.

Eighty percent of Australians over 65 are on a pension, 60% of Australian families pay no net tax, and 20% of Australian youth are unemployed. Forty-two percent of Labor (ALP) lower-house MPs and 71% of ALP upper-house MPs are ex-union. The national executive of the ALP has 73% of its members from unions.

The end result: the unions have members that represent 12% of the voting age. Well over 50% of the voting age are reliant on the government for their income. The unions have a $15 billion a year fighting fund.

Where is the power?

15. The tortoise and the hare

In all areas, the tortoise normally wins in the long run. Those kids at school for which it came easy. Where are they today? But more importantly why? It all came too easily and then suddenly they were confronted by others that had spent years of hard work getting it right. Malcolm Gladwell defined the concept of 10,000 hours. Do something for 10,000 hours and you get good at it. The same theory applies to things you buy. A machine that goes straight to work is a dream. But when it goes wrong, how do you handle it. Those machines that are hard to commission often turn out to be the best because you know how to operate them. I guess the same applies to people. Some relationships just seem to hit it off, but then things go wrong and you do not know how to handle it. Those that are prickly at the start often end up the best, because you know how to deal with the complications of the

16. Our moral structure has moved from church to courtroom

As Church attendance slows the moral framework of our culture has moved to the Courtroom. Instead of relying on the Church to define what is right and what is wrong we have allowed government to write our moral compass into legislation and regulations. In 2012, we wrote more legislation in a 12-month period than was written in the first 50 years of Federation, eclipsing the mass of legislation created each year before and after. The result has been the eruption of judicial differences resulting for the first time in public brawling not unlike what occurred in churches over a period. It will be interesting to see if the disruption to the Queensland Supreme Court and the Human Rights Commission continues in other judicial arenas.

17. The four seasons

Every project has four seasons just as the weather has four seasons.

Winter. The ground is frozen and the nights are long. This is the time for dreaming and planning. During the long nights, you can let your imagination run riot and truly think laterally. It is also a time to plan.

Spring. This is the season of hard work. The plans need to be put into place. There is a need for hard work on a daily basis.

Summer. Lets you look at the growth while feeding and cultivating.

Autumn. The time to reap the harvest.

The ideal in life is to have four projects going at any one time. One project in each of the phases. This allows you to share between your creative side and hard work. It also lets you witness the joy of harvest while doing the hard work on the next project.

18. Solutions to problems and good feelings

Fifteen years ago, I read a book that said that you only sold two things. Solutions to problems and good feelings. I have been trying to find a business for which that is not true. So far, no go. Solve someone's problem and leave them feeling good about it. Of course, that is the opposite of what happens in most businesses today. How many times do you contact a business and are greeted with this smiling voice that asks all these wonderful questions. They go through the process but have no way to solve your problem or remove the frustration. We have become a procedure driven society that goes through the process but who cares about the outcome?

19. Perceptions are real

People develop very strong perceptions at an early age, and they stick to those perceptions. The first time I confronted this was in university. I had been in a study group for 3 years with about 20 people. We went on a geological excursion and ended up staying in some shearers' quarters. One night we were sitting around talking about all sorts of things and the subject of schools came up. It got a bit heated. I was standing against a wall when someone announced I had gone to a private school. This one guy came at me and threw me through the fibro wall, before I had the faintest idea what was happening. I had worked with him for 3 years and we had no problem, but when he found out I went to a private school he lost it and never talked to me again. Perceptions are real.

20. Money does weird things to people

I don't care who you are or where you come from, money screws the mind. I have seen it with friendships. We lost a few when we moved into a more affluent suburb. I have seen it in business, employees wanting to sue us for giving them heaps but not enough. I have seen it in sports stars and others. Over 90% of lotto winners throughout the world end up worse off in ten years. Money does weird things to people.

21. Failure is not only building, it is good

What do successful people do more than everybody else, they fail. They fail more simply because they do more. During the 2016 US presidential elections the worst thing that some people could say about Donald Trump was that he had been a bankrupt. Look through the biographies of truly successful people and you will find them full of failures. In many cases the entrepreneurs don't survive, but those that do take on board the lessons and then have another go. There are numerous phoenix stories and I suggest you read some.

Failure is not only good because it allows you to build from a loss but it is also good in that it opens your eyes to the risks around you. I have noted in the political section that most politicians today are either lawyers or political staffers. They have had no experience in putting all they have at risk. Once you have done that a few times you tend to look at the world through different glasses. You start to know when to cut your losses and when to hang in there.

Do not be afraid of failure, learn from it and let it strengthen you. When I first went to a serious water skiing training session someone came out of the water and said, "I haven't fallen off today", and a champion walking past just said "well, you haven't been trying".

22. Balance

It always has been and always will be a question of balance. The problem is that there are so many things to balance. So how do we balance all of them together? (The process for doing this will be defined later in problem-solving.) After going through the problem-solving process, I came up with five major elements that need to be balanced one against the other. You may disagree, and if you do I would love to change my group. Life is a balance of: lifestyle, career satisfaction, finances, kudos and morals/ethics. These will be discussed separately later. So hold judgment until you have read them all and see how they mix and match with each other and your world.

23. Lifestyle varies from the old hippies to those totally obsessed with the fast lane

It is a function of where you live, what you do, and your relationship with your family, friends and colleagues. It also varies from narcissism and egocentric behaviour through to altruism and unselfish behaviour. Within lifestyle there is a balance between being a carefree personality through to an obsessive personality. Lifestyle is a function of where you live, how you live and with whom you live. A few friends or many friends? Lifestyle is about the way you live your style, attitudes and possessions. Charles Handy stated that the three stages of life in the early 20th century will turn into five stages in the 21st century. Those five stages are education, career, teaching, mentoring, retirement. Each stage needs a different lifestyle. We have not been trained to think about our lifestyle let alone plan it and control it. It tends to just happen.

24. Career satisfaction is something needed and in fact demanded by many

However, to others a job is a source of income that supplies their financial needs for their lifestyle. For a job to be satisfying it needs to challenge, it needs to excite and it needs to satisfy the emotional needs. Never forget every job is the same after 6 months. Every job is repetitive, so you had better like the repetition.

25. Finance

If you earn a dollar more than you spend there is no pressure. If you earn a dollar less than you spend the pressure builds. Therefore, finance is a function of your needs versus your earnings. This is related to lifestyle, morals and kudos, however overall the amount you need to earn is a function of your financial needs and your ability to budget. During your life, your income will change from unearned as a child, to earned as an adult to unearned in retirement. These changes need to be managed. There will be three major expenses in your life that will need time, skill and planning to achieve. The first is the building or buying of your home, the second is the education of your family and the third is the funding of your retirement. Success will come from maximising the amount you save, the time over which you save and the return you get on your savings. The amount you save requires will power and discipline. The timeframe requires the development of goals and planning, and the return you get on your portfolio requires skill, patience and discipline. I define wealth as having a dollar more in unearned income each year than your lifestyle requires. If you can achieve that the balancing act becomes that much easier.

26. *Kudos is sometimes the most difficult parameter to understand*

There are some that are totally obsessed with what others think; others could not care less. Peer pressure can be uplifting; it can also be totally destructive.

Kudos is the praise or honour we seek for an achievement. How much are we doing what we do for ourselves, how much for praise from parents, peers, children or the public in general? We seek kudos in our families, our careers and our general life. Are we doing something to make ourselves or others feel good? If we do something for others are we doing it for them or for us? Where is the balance? If we do it for ourselves we are being selfish, if we are doing it for others, is it for the kudos or for them, asking nothing in return.

This subject is so closely linked to the moral or ethical principles by which we operate, it is hard to distinguish them. The kudos element is more a function of ethics as it relates to how we interact with our families and our communities. The desire to be loved, praised and honoured can drive many people to do some really dumb things. It drives the decisions on where we live, what car we drive, what clothes we wear and how we do our hair.

To understand our link with others we need to understand ourselves. A 1996 survey of employees by Harvard University put positive customer feedback as the major reward required for motivation. Today it is hard to get through a meal without hearing "great work or good job", and it is well known that Gen Y need constant stroking to perform. People need praise and honour, not enough is harmful and too much is harmful. You need to balance your need for kudos with the needs of others.

27. Morals/ethics

This whole subject has been redefined over the last century. Certainly, until the beginning of the 20th century both morals and ethics were defined for us by the Church. But the Church has lost its influence and therefore the definition of morals has come down to teachers and parents.

In relation to ethics, as with morals, the Church used to define the rules of behaviour, however their place has been taken by the judiciary. There are two problems for children these days. The first is defining the moral standards for themselves and the second is to redefine their ethical behaviour.

The judiciary has made ethical standards that are in complete contradiction to personal moral standards. Morals have been based on our duties and responsibilities as a Christian. Ethical standards are being judged on rights and not responsibilities. There is no benchmark anymore. One could argue that the judiciary took over from the Church because the Church was too slow to move with the times. Or you could argue that the judiciary has moved too quickly in transferring responsibility for actions from moral responsibilities to legal rights.

Whichever way you look at the situation it has become increasingly difficult for people to understand their moral obligations, and sometimes impossible to understand their legal responsibilities. The latest one I have been looking at is *Dallas Buyers Club*. There is no doubt that thousands of people stole the movie with the help of their internet service providers (ISPs). They got caught. But the ISPs argue that it is legally or ethically wrong for them to have to give up the names of the people who stole the movie.

In the old days that would be harbouring a fugitive, today it is the ethical right of the thief to hide behind their "right to privacy". Therefore, the judiciary is saying it is ethical to hide information that would lead to a conviction. That used to be the province of lawyers and spouses, then it went to other professionals and now to ISPs. As the judiciary makes the new ethical rules, they become less like our moral rules. We all have to make up our minds whether we want to act morally or ethically. Sounds a bit like the old Godfather mentality. One set of rules for the family (morals), and another for business (ethics.) Nothing personal!

28. The growth curve

I was introduced to the hockey stick graph many years ago. It shows the rate at which people grow. It can be used for learning, for fitness, weight loss and many other things.

The outstanding feature is that the vast majority of people, after setting themselves goals, give up just before the high growth period starts. 50% of new businesses do not make it through the first year, 50% of the successful ones fail before the end of the second year, and so on. 30% of tertiary students crash out before finishing. I read today 50% of new dental graduates will struggle to get a job. And of course, 80% of those aged 65+have resorted to the pension. So I have learned. Firstly, people give up too early. Secondly our society is now accepting of those that give up.

29. Survival attained, the drive to achieve disappears

Once survival has been attained, the drive to achieve disappears for most people, or it is simply that the direction is undefined.

It used to annoy me and then frustrate me that the vast majority of the population have very little idea of their objectives. It was only a hundred years ago that the vast majority of people lived to survive. Now that government has assured survival, what is the purpose of living? Some would say to procreate, well what next. Many philosophers have struggled with the meaning of life, but that was the luxury of a few, now it is the duty of all. Humans used to get one shot. Now you get three or four.

30. You always need a Plan B

In every biography or book about success there is normally a lot of words but a few gems to take home. The gem I took from *The Art of The Deal*, was do not just have Plan A, but also Plan B and Plan C. An Uncle bought a cliff top block on the cliff overlooking the sea. There was only about ten metres of land at the road level and then the land dropped off over a cliff. There was about 40 metres of land at the base of the cliff going down to the water's edge. The Uncle employed an architect to draw up a counter levered house that sat on the top of the cliff. When he was showing me the plans he also had plans for another house built into the cliff below the first house. He said that was in case he ran out of money with the first house, he could sell it and build the second one below.

The restaurant business has been huge in the last decade or more in Australia, yet it costs a small fortune to design and build a kitchen. If you pour all that capital into infrastructure you need a plan B to get the capital back. Most restaurant owners have no plan B and therefore the capital is lost.

31. You can't make a silk purse out of a sow's ear

In his autobiography, Lee Iacocca tells the story about the Henry Ford hamburger. Henry Ford II always said that the best hamburger in the word could be found in the Ford dining room. When he travelled around the world, many chefs tried to take the title of best hamburger, but none did. After he died Iacocca went to the head chef in the Ford dining room and asked the secret. The answer came back. "Well you go to the cool room and pull out the best piece of scotch filet steak…" Great ingredients are always needed for great dishes. When you try to upgrade poor raw material you very quickly come to the point of a diminishing return.

Having said that, my business partner and I made a huge success of making an average product out of very low grade raw material. We solved a problem and left them feeling good.

32. Work towards getting paid for what you can do, not what you do

When you are young and energetic you feel invincible and that you will be able to go forever. So longevity is not an issue. You also think that you love what you do and that love will go on forever. I hate to burst the bubble

Many friends who are professionals have not been able to get away because they are not earning if they are not there doing whatever it is that they do. A doctor, lawyer, dentist, architect doesn't get paid if they do not work. But those who build a business structure get paid whether they are there or not.

I have already told the story of the maintenance guys at the APM mill in Melbourne. They got paid only when there was a breakdown. So they were paid because they could fix it, not because they were fixing it. The other way of getting paid for what you can do is to get on a retainer in your field of expertise.

Carpet layers all burn out early with bad knees. Air traffic controllers burn out from stress. Many professions have a use-by date. You need to get yourself in a position where people will pay you for your expertise even when you are not actually doing it.

33. Problem-solving

1. Define the problem
2. Quantify it
3. List all the causes
4. Categorise
5. Prioritise

6. Define the vision of where you need to change to
7. Measure where you are
8. Create a plan to achieve your goals
9. Implement the plan
10. Measure where you have gone

The vast majority of people skip to step 9 before even defining the problem. This leads to solving the wrong problem. Or they conclude the cause of the problem without clearly defining it and therefore fix a symptom instead of a cause.

34. When delegating, make sure the responsibility lies with one person

If there is shared responsibility the project will not get done and the information tends to be deposited all over the place. If two people have responsibility for the same key performance indicator (KPI), then they will both demand praise in times of good performance and they will both run a mile when it all goes pear-shaped.

35. Government and 1st tier business capital projects are costing three times what they need to

The swing to socialism had brought with it a huge increase in the cost of doing things. In the 1970s larger companies bought up a whole lot of small companies run by families or sole entrepreneurs. They looked at the smaller companies and thought we can do this so much better, well they couldn't. The reality was that small and medium-sized enterprises (SMEs) are far more productive than bigger companies. The big companies found this out as the years went by and had to close or offload many of the purchases. This trait has continued on its merry way. Large corporations are like governments, they have so many rules and procedures it makes every task more difficult and more costly than it should be. These large corporations have done deals with the unions and government so that they end up paying a lot more than they should. On top of that theft and fraud is a major problem. When Parliament House was being built, I was flying from Sydney to Brisbane seated next to an engineer on the building team. He asked me how many toilet cisterns were delivered to the work site, I said I had no idea. He answers was "About twice as many as were installed."

In government projects, by the time there is the planning to plan, the plans and the specifications and drawings and licenses and legals, the cost is often greater before the first shovel hits the dirt than it would cost for a small business to do the whole job. Of course, today you cannot get a government contract if you are not a preferred supplier and that costs big time.

(At the time of editing the Royal Commission into the Banks and Financial Institutions is starting to lift the lid and the extra costs that we have been paying.)

36. The 6 Ps. Proper Planning Prevents Piss Poor Performance

It doesn't matter if you are going down to the store to get groceries or building a ten-story building, if you do not plan it properly it is almost guaranteed to fail. But today there does appear to be back up after back up, but not always. The Japanese flew ahead of the rest of the world in the 1980s through the principles of zero defects. W. Edwards Deming was an American engineer and management consultant that had to go to Japan because the Americans did not believe in his principles. As a result, the Japanese far surpassed the Americans in manufacturing technology. One of his quotes was "If you can't describe what you are doing as a process, you don't know what you are doing." That has proved to be true and needs to be understood. Whatever you do must be planned and documented so that you know exactly what it is you are going to do.

You need a study diary or you have no structure. You need to make sure all your devices are charged when you need them.

37. Ways of thinking

In number one the need for teamwork was recognised. Within that team there is a need for balance in the participants. There is also a necessity for the way of thinking.

Entrepreneurs think about the goal. They have complete belief in the fact that they are going to get there, and nothing will get in their way.

The technicians think about how it works. Their minds go to what makes it work and what is necessary to keep it working.

The administrator thinks about process and what happened. The administrator has two roles. The first is to document what is about to happen and what is happening, the other is the role of the historian, what has happened.

What has occurred in our society over the last few decades is that all these functions have had the legal mind superimposed over them. The legal mind thinks of two things: precedent and apportionment of blame. What has happened in the past and who is to blame for it. This way of thinking results in further regulations to clarify the apportionment of blame in the future.

If the entrepreneur rules the process gets too risky and often fails. If the administrator gets too strong the process is slowed and the efficiency reduced. If the technician is in control it is all about the making, or the service provision and the focus on the customer disappears

The problem, then, is how does this fit with the rule that says there must be one person in charge. The answer to that is the person in charge must be astute enough to manage all the different ways of thinking and to mould them into the best fit.

If you want evidence have a look at all the successful organisations you know, I will bet there is a mixture of skills, thought patterns and there will be a distribution of power.

38. A leader that has no followers is just someone taking a walk

I have often thought while writing this manual that I am just taking a walk. The vast majority of the population think the whole concept of planning your life and making a lifetime plan to finance your house, education and retirement is stark raving mad. Because this is a lifetime project it is even harder to get people to understand and follow the rules. It is important to question your direction whether you have followers or not. That is why it is important to understand your values and principles because then you can walk alone if need be.

39. Do the hardest things first

Now this can been seen as a direct contradiction of the John Gray adage. In *Venus and Mars*, John Gray talks about points and the fact that women keep count. He goes on to say that in a woman's mind a man gets one point for every job. Therefore, if there are ten things we need to do starting with painting the house and working down to putting out the rubbish, you get the same point for each task. Painting the house takes days, doing the minor jobs takes minutes. Men always want to do the big tasks first and as a result leave all the little ones undone. This works against men in the scoring system.

What we are talking about here is at the other end of the spectrum. There will be times in your life when you feel as though the walls are coming down on you. You will have a myriad of tasks on your plate and they are dragging you down to the point where you are frozen. It is at those times that you need to make a list of all the issues from hardest at the top to lowest at the bottom. You then need to attack the hardest issue. In most cases once the top two issues are dealt with the rest seem to just fade away, but if you spend your time dealing with the lightweight issues the hard ones never get dealt with and you continue to feel all that pressure.

40. Eat breakfast like a king, lunch like a prince and dinner like a pauper

You need to eat in the morning to feed the engine for the day. If you eat a heavy meal at night then you go to bed with your stomach working overtime, not good. And finally, if you go to bed on an empty stomach then your body burns fat all night, and you do not feel hungry.

41. The gut buster

Gary Egger suggests in his book *Gut Buster* that if you increase your heart rate to 120–130 bpm for 20 mins that will increase your metabolism for the next 8 hours. That means 20 mins quick walking and you benefit from more burnt calories for the next 8 hours. Over the years, I have heard so many stories of this being true.

42. Routine

Every parent knows how important routines are to kids, even our dogs know to the nearest 5 minutes when it is dinner time and they don't have a watch/phone and they can't read. Yet we seem to think that routine can go out the door as soon as we become adults.

Recent studies show that even the sleep hours are important. Go to bed at the same time and get up at the same time.

There are many reasons for routine being so important.
- We can only get the most out of our day if we plan it, and routine makes planning easier. Ask anyone who has to do rosters. You start with the old one and make as few changes as you can.
- Automation. If we have a routine we can do many tasks on automatic, less thinking more productivity.
- Getting over the grind. This is the one I like most.

We all have tasks we do not like doing. Whether it's putting the rubbish out, marking assessments or wading through correspondence, we need a special push to get us through the task we do not want to do, yet we have to do them week after week after week. A routine makes the decision easy. If you procrastinate then it is likely to get left out. But if you allocate a certain time for that activity you will find you can achieve it quickly and with the minimum of pain.

Different people have different routines, it depends on your personality. Do not try to copy another person's routine. I had one friend who planned his next day in bullet points before going to bed. Another that did that task over breakfast. The morning person said they would have been up all night worrying if they had done the task the night before.

43. One of the most important lessons in life

God, grant me the serenity to accept
the things I cannot change,
Courage to change the things I can,
And wisdom to know the difference.
—Reinhold Niebuhr

In other words, pick your fights. When you are young and have boundless energy, you can fight on many fronts at once. However, as you grow your energy levels will drop and you have to learn to pick the fights worth having. I have been with my wife for 35 years now. It was not the first marriage for either of us. A few years into the marriage someone said that they had never seen us fight and how is that possible. We both thought about it for a while and both answered. "When the going gets tough, we figure out who has the most vested in that particular fight, and the other one backs off." That is a really important lesson. Do not waste energy on fights you do not have to put energy into.

44. What goes around comes around

This is tied to the third law of motion. "For every action there is an equal and opposite reaction". The saying means that if you start something it is likely to come back to you at some stage.

45. The pendulum does swing

In my last years of school, branding hit the market place. By the late 1960s clothes started to have labels on the outside. This had never been heard of before. Many people refused to wear such clothing as they were advertising the brand by wearing it. Shock Horror. 30 years later I put two shirts up to a bunch of 30-year-olds and asked them which one they would wear. They nearly all said the one with the logo even though it was three times the price. Today I read that attitudes to shopping are changing in the states and people will no longer pay for branded clothes. The wheel goes around.

Another good example is when a family member had a child and was told that if the child was not breast fed that it would not achieve its full potential. The mother was terrified of the "lactation Nazi" nurse to the point that she had to be sent home before her milk would come down. On the birthing of her next child she had the same nurse. But this time feeding was at the discretion of the mother.

Sometimes you just have to stay in the same place and wait for the pendulum to swing back to you.

46. Do today's work today

Sounds simple, but for so many it is so hard.

Some people write lists of what they are going to do tomorrow every night. They normally get it done. We have talked about written goals are normally achieved, well this is a good example of that.

I'll finish it tomorrow means that there is something else

tomorrow that will not get done and you will live in a world where you are constantly getting behind.

If you plan to do something today, do it today, do not put it off until tomorrow.

47. There is no recovery

After cyclone Yasi, we spent many years cleaning up the mess and working with others that had been through disasters. Society and the media talk about recovery. Let me tell you there is no recovery from disaster. Recovery is defined as returning to a normal state of health, mind or strength. The reason there is no recovery after a disaster is that you never return to where you were. You either grow and become much stronger and develop a new norm or you weaken and never regain that normal state of health or mind.

I feel saddened when I hear that a town or a company or a country has recovered, because I know it is not true. There are many like the Twin Towers, Chernobyl and Fukushima that obviously will never recover. But then there are the ones that nobody knows about. Cardwell did a lot of work with the rebuilders of Marysville. I think they were about 18 months ahead of us but we were going down the same path.

Marysville was a town that had its heyday many years before the fire. The traditional businesses in town were losing their gloss and it was fast becoming a retirement town. When 80% of the town was burnt and we hear that it has recovered there is a mental picture of new houses and vibrant families and businesses, all not true. What happened in Marysville is the same that happens in most places where there is disaster and no great driving force to rebuild. At a personal level the devastation is immense.

The same happened in Cardwell. The population went from 1500 to 800 in a month, and there is nothing to grow it. The industries that built the town have been shut down and a new industry is yet to grow.

On a personal level, what happens is that you have a family living in a $350,000 home. It is destroyed or burnt to the ground. The insurance pays up, no problem. So there you are without a home, without a job and $350,000. It is going to take at least a year to rebuild, so you have to support yourself during that time, so you do not have $350,000 to spend, you only have $300,000.

You go to a builder and ask for the house to be rebuilt. Of course, since your house was built the building standards have changed and now for the same amount of money you get half the house you used to live in. You are then confronted with the decision to rebuild half the house you had, get a loan and rebuild your house or move to another area.

All three options are not very palatable. You do not want to live in a house half of what you are used to, in middle age the last thing you want to do is put a new mortgage around your neck, and moving away from home is not a great option. Nevertheless, the vast majority of people move, and hence the town never recovers.

48. *You can teach an old dog new tricks*

As you grow older change becomes more difficult, not impossible. Children learn quickly whether it is a new language or a new skill. For adults the process is more difficult but not impossible. If there is something about you that you feel needs to change, get yourself a goal and put a plan in place and it can happen.

49. *You cannot regulate or legislate against bad behaviour*

First religions and then governments have tried to regulate against bad behaviour. The Christian faith brought out the ten commandments backed up by The Bible in an attempt to reinforce the laws with values. Other religions have tried in their own way to enforce behavioural standards through punishment.

When governance changed from the church to government, lawyers got involved and delivered a myriad of legislation that has had little or no effect on bad behaviour. In fact, I think it is fair to say that the sharper the definition of bad behaviour, the easier it is to get around the legislation.

Society needs to find a better way of controlling behaviour. In the meantime, all we can do is sit and watch as the lawyers write more and more legislation with little or no effect.

Tell a child not to do something and they will have an uncontrollable desire to do it. *Explain* why they should not do something and you have a chance.

50. Values are at the heart of our lives

As our knowledge as a society grows and technology moves on, it is becoming easier to be hoodwinked, conned or just plain manipulated. When others are trying to persuade you, it is important to relate the information to your value base. Without a clear set of values, either groupthink or linguistic constructivism can lead you to the dark side before you know what has happened.

51. True happiness always comes from outside your comfort zone

Sitting around bingeing on TV programs, movies, video games, alcohol, drugs, music or exercise does not get you true happiness. That only comes from when you step outside your comfort zone push yourself into zones you thought you would never achieve.

52. Everybody wants to be useful

It has been built into our DNA over 600,000 years to survive. However in the world today only 8.4% are considered to live in poverty so that means 91.6% of the world does not need to use its basic reason for life. What we do need is to be useful. A life without use is a life without meaning. The greatest use you can have in society is to be self reliant and not be burden on others.

5
Finance

Finance is the way in which money is used and handled. From what we saw in the political equation, finance has a very important part in society. There are the issues of who controls the capital, how the wealth is shared around and how transactions take place. To understand finance, we need to understand what money is and why we have it. We need to know how to store it, save it and count it.

Money

Money is a medium of exchange that is used to simplify transactions as it has a unit of value associated with it. Before money there was barter. There are two major theories of how money came about. Aristotle considered every object had two values, the first being the original purpose and the second being the possibility of use in barter, that is exchange for another object. The other theory brings in the concept of services. You do something for someone and they "owe you one". The question became one what. So was born the gift economy, where if someone had an object or service someone else wanted, they would gift it to them in exchange for an IOU, which later became money.

Precious metals

The first clear form of money was precious metals, after the use of livestock. This morphed into the use of silver and gold first as metals and later as coins. Using the metals by themselves required the weighing of the metal for each use. This was replaced by the pre-weighing of coins.

Coins

The next step was changing from using the coins as a unit of weight to a unit of value.

Bills of exchange

Traveling with currency was difficult for safety reasons as well as for logistical reasons. As a result, bills of exchange were introduced. This is when a trader buys a product from a supplier and instead of paying money in the form of coins they would pay with a promissory note. The note was a guarantee of payment. That may have worked well for those that trusted each other, but in the main it needed an intermediary who would guarantee the note. The intermediary would be an entity that was regarded by all. The notes had several benefits. 1. They allowed secure payment. 2. The note might be for 90 days but the bearer could cash it sooner for a discount. 3. The notes could travel from town to town.

Banknotes

Firstly issued by banks or trading houses partially backed by gold and partially by reputation. Then banknotes issued by governments. These were theoretically convertible to gold or silver and now just guaranteed by the government.

Cryptocurrencies

The latest development including blockchain technology and bitcoins. A few decades ago, the thought of cash going from our economy was ridiculous. It now appears that money in general may disappear from our financial system and be replaced by cryptocurrencies. It was reported recently that blockchain technology will take the place of CHESS in the equities market, so hang on to your hats for the changes in this area.

Conclusion

We have done the full circle. Starting with an exchange of something of value from one peer to another in a transaction. The monetary system was then guided through a maze of intermediaries who all wanted their cut out of a transaction. And now we are going back to peer to peer transactions with no intermediary.

The value of money

We value goods and services in monetary terms, but how do we value money? It is easy to put a value on what money can buy. We all know what food, clothing and entertainment cost in terms of money. But few of us work out what housing, electricity, insurance and council rates cost. These are things that will be addressed in budgeting.

How many can say what a unit of money costs? If you have $1,000 dollars in your account, what did it cost to put it there? The average university graduate will commence work on a salary of about $55,000 per year. That works out at about $30 per hour at work. Now you have to pay tax on that, so it becomes about $27 per hour.

That makes it easy to relate to purchases with money. You can say that if a shirt costs one two or three hours' work. You go out to dinner and that costs so many hours' work. How does that relate to cars, houses, insurance and rates? If the council rates are $4,000 per year that relates to 148 hours of work or nearly four weeks. A $27,000 car is 1,000 hours of work or six months. Electricity in an average home is about $4,000 per year, the mortgage on a $300,000 home loan would be $1,448 per month or 54 hours or 6.7 days. Food at $108 per week is four hours. Rent at $216 per week is eight hours. So we can balance the value that money buys with the value of what it takes to earn the money.

You may ask, why bother with all this? The answer is simple.

There are so many products out there, so many ways of solving issues, it is hard to pick the right one if you don't understand exactly what it is that you are doing. So this is an exercise of understanding the basic elements of what you are trying to achieve; that way there is a better chance that you will put in place products and processes that achieve your aims and not somebody else's.

Storing money

You may think that storing money is pretty simple, but the reality is that it is very difficult. What type of account do you want or need? You need to balance—that word again—the interest rate with liquidity and security.

Under the bed

You know where it is. There is a security risk if you are robbed. It will be the same when you come to collect it in 12 months' time.

In the bank

That used to be a simple matter, now it is a lot more difficult as the bank has so many products that it wants to sell you. The advantages of leaving it in the bank are:

1. It is safe.
2. You can earn interest on it. Putting money in the bank is not as easy as it used to be. Years ago, you opened a savings account. These days there are many different types of accounts. These accounts vary in the interest rate that they pay depending on the access to your money, and the amount you have in the account.

Other investments

This is a subject we will deal with later.

Saving money

The concept of saving is simple, it is the amount that you earn greater than the amount you have spent in each period. Therefore, if you earn $100 per week and spend $80 per week you have saved $20. The question then becomes what to do with the savings. In this instance, we have a chicken and an egg problem. Should you save and then figure out what to do with it, or should you develop a savings plan and then work to the plan? A little bit of advice. "Targets are more likely to get hit than dreams." The best way to save is to start with a goal. What are you saving for? When is the money required? Targets. Human nature loves achieving targets. Set yourself a goal and you will want to achieve it. If you just go out for a run you are likely to run around the block and then be home in ten minutes. If you say to yourself I am going to run for 30 mins a day 4 days a week, then there is a goal that you can achieve and probably will. All good goals should have a quantity and a timeframe, without those two, goals are just simply motherhood statements that mean nothing. The strength of the goal is important. A weak goal is not worth the effort. With a goal too far away it is easy to say, "Oh that goal was always too hard so no big deal if I do not make it." The goal must be measured. Later, we will talk about stretch targets but for now let's focus on setting workable goals.

Income as a function of saving

Many people make the mistake of thinking that you need a big income to save. Not so. In fact, many people on big incomes find it hard to save because they get so caught up in borrowing money to reduce tax that they lose sight of the bigger picture.

Vehicle

Banks have many products and you must choose the right vehicle for the road on which you are to travel. In the initial stages, you need to choose the right account. Many think this is an easy decision because if you make a mistake it is easily fixed later. As we will discuss time and again in the process of investing strategy, structure and rate of return are all important factors. You need to get the structure correct early. These days changing a bank account can become a time consuming, expensive and difficult job. If you set up a savings account and then later start investing in equities and property, you will have income coming into that account. If you need to change the account, you will need to change the information on all the documentation in relation to all your investments. At this stage that doesn't seem like a big deal but later it will become just that. Now is time for one of those learning moments. "Murphy's Law is real." If you have not planned well ahead the chances of those moments when everything goes wrong together is significantly increased. Stephen Covey in his seven habits talks about beginning with the end in mind. This is extremely important when setting up your structure.

Budgeting

We said that saving was the result of earning more than you spend. We also said that written goals are more likely to be achieved. The mechanism to achieve a written savings goal starts with the budget. You need to get a simple spreadsheet or piece of paper, divide it down the middle and write all the income of the left-hand side and all the expenses on the right-hand side. You then add up both sides and the difference will be your savings. The trick to budgeting is to write in the amount you want to save first and then leave it there. You can then play with the income and expenses to achieve your objective.

Counting money: accounting

Counting money is a really important part of the finance process, it is even more important when we come to investing. What is the point of a goal if you are not measuring where you are in relation to the goal?

The next point is one that is really important, often not understood, and even more often not realised or acknowledged.

There are two types of accounting. The first is financial accounting and the second is management accounting. 95% of accountants are historians, they simply tell the story of what happened. You will remember from the video, on the introduction to the economy, that the economy starts with the transaction which is the building block of the financial world. The financial accounts simply take all those transactions, list them, categorise them and then let them tell the story of what happened. In the industry jargon, financial accounting is the field concerned with the summary, analysis and reporting of financial transactions pertaining to a business. It involves the preparation of financial statements.

A management accountant works out where the costs are and how to work the system to make it more productive in the future. Management accounting is the process of identifying, measuring, analysing, interpreting and communicating information for the pursuit of the organisation's goals.

There is the difference. The management accountant is part of the team that helps you play the game, the financial accountant is the person who puts the scores on the board.

Both have really important jobs. Most people fall into the trap of thinking a financial accountant is part of the team, they are only the scorer. Many investors have lost huge amounts getting these roles mixed up.

Profit and loss

The P&L statement is a statement of income minus expenses over a period of time, normally an accounting period, and that gives you your profit.

As usual, nothing is as simple as you think. There are many different definitions of income and expenses. Once again, you need to learn the language before you can delve into the subject.

This is really boring stuff, but it is important you get a grasp of it so that you can learn to read the fantasy works that companies put out in the name of financial statements.

And if you do not believe that most of this is fantasy, try reading a Federal Budget.

Income

Corporate income

When we talk about corporate income, we are talking about you as a corporation or a trust or a SMSF, even you in a super fund.

What does income mean? There are many definitions of income: gross income, tax assessable income, net income, after-tax income. Later you can get into EBIT, and EBITA and many others.

These are all measures that have applications in certain situations but are mostly there to confuse the issue. The job of a CEO is to reinvest the earnings of a company. The CEO is only interested in the amount of cash they have in their hands to either pay out as dividends to their shareholders or reinvest to get a higher return. Your job is the same. You are only interested in the amount of cash you have after all income and expenses are counted. Therefore, income needs to be defined as net income after all expenses and tax. This means that tax must be considered in the income equation. You cannot afford to think you have saved a certain amount only to find you have tax to pay. On the other hand, if you have a refund coming your way, you need to know about it.

Personal income

When we talk about personal income that is you as a tax entity.

Earned income

Income that you have earned as a reward for your endeavours. Earned income has two major components. Income earned from what you actually do today and income earned for what you may be able to do. It is better to find a job where you get paid for what you can do rather than what you do do.

Unearned income

Income that you have received because of an investment, or as a function of something you did in the past, not what you are doing today.

Back in ancient history, when there was manufacturing in Australia, I went to the APM mill in Melbourne where they made paper. This was a factory about 1km long that started with a slurry and ended up with massive rolls of paper weighing tonnes. In the middle of the factory was this huge machine that rolled the paper. In a heated room—we were in Melbourne—there sat half a dozen men playing cards. Someone asked what they were doing and the manager said they were the maintenance staff. The same person asked how the manager felt paying them to sit there and do nothing for the company. He replied saying he was delighted.

We all looked a bit puzzled. He then went on to say that the machine they were responsible for made the company $10,000 per hour, and therefore if it stopped the company was losing $10,000 per hour. The six men, remember this is in the 1960s, cost the company less than $100 per hour. Therefore, the more they sat there and played cards the better he liked it. That is one example of getting paid for what you can do rather than what you do do.

Another example is when people are put on a retainer, they get paid for being on call. To some extent, top-line professionals get paid for what they can do. If you think of a top-of-the-line doctor or lawyer, you pay them $800 per hour not because of what they actually do for you but more for what they might see that others may miss.

The point is that as you get older, it becomes harder and harder to actually do the physical and mental stuff that you did 30 years ago, therefore you want to slowly change from earned income to unearned income.

There is a huge number of sources of income: interest, dividends, franking credits, coupon rates, rent and leases, and each of these have a number of factors affecting them. This is not a book on finance; it is trying to show you where to look to get the answers you need. At some stage, you will open an online broking account; nearly all of these have online material that gives the background to the language of finance. You will need to get hold of that material and make yourself familiar with the language.

Expenses

When you are drawing up your budget, the expense column needs to be divided into essential and non-essential items. Rent, electricity, food, rates and insurance are all essential items. Fashion clothing and accessories, entertainment and treats are all non-essential. The budgeting process is not about stopping spending on non-essentials, it is about understanding what you are doing.

As with the time budget above, I have allowed for 20 hours a week for fun and play. That is 3 hours a day. I believe an average of 3 hours a day of frivolous activity is enough. More is overkill and less could make you dull and boring.

Expenses need to be categorised. 35-year-olds today are saying they cannot afford houses. They are not thinking about the years of non-essential expenses that could have bought that house for them. That the average person spends $15 on lunch instead of making it at home for $3. That is $12 per day or over $4,000 per year. And all those $5 coffees. It is hard to put an old head on young shoulders. However, it doesn't take a genius to know that all these non-essential expenses over ten years can make an incredible difference.

Cash flow

Most bankruptcies do not result from negative balance sheets or even negative P&Ls. They result from the fact that the person does not have the cash, that is money, to pay their bills. There are the items that either come or go once a year that can really throw the whole equation on its head. To get around this there are plenty of people willing to lend you money to pay the big one-offs. That money comes at a huge cost. There are also many that will offer for you to pay monthly, quarterly or yearly. You will note that paying in instalments normally ends up costing a lot more than the one-off yearly payment. When you are doing your budget, you need to also do a cash flow analysis so that you have the money on hand to pay your bills when they are due.

Balance sheet

While the P&L is a video of what happened over a period of time, a balance sheet is a single snapshot of the assets, liabilities and capital of a business at a particular point in time.

Here, again, we have to remember the two different types of accounting. The financial accountant prepares a balance sheet as a historian and for the ATO. The management accountant prepares a balance sheet to give you an idea of how you are actually doing. In my role as a business consultant, every balance sheet I was shown lead me to the same conclusion: that the company was in real trouble. (Nobody asks for help until it is far too late.) The owners would say, "but the balance sheet says I am a millionaire." Well sorry, your accountant had put a new valuation on the building, a director's valuation that was about double what it is worth. Your plant and equipment is valued at cost minus depreciation, when in fact if you wanted to sell it you couldn't give it away, and you haven't allowed for the clean-up if you get out of these premises. This is not a lecture on accounting; it is a lesson in telling the story for what you want, not what someone else thinks you want.

Taxation

Personal Income Tax	Your taxable income is your total income including dividends and capital gains less your deductions.
Company Tax	In Australia, the company tax rate is 30% of taxable income. Recent changes have been made. This is ongoing so you will need to verify the correct tax rate for different entities by checking this on the Australian Tax Office webpage: www.ato.gov.au
Franking Credits	When a company makes a profit, it pays tax on that profit. So, in effect, the dividend it pays to the shareholder has already had tax paid on it. The franking credit is a recognition of that tax paid. When the recipient receives the franking credit, it is added to the overall income and also added to the amount of tax already paid. This avoids double taxation. If a company makes a $1000 profit it pays $300 tax to the ATO. The company then pays a 10% dividend to the shareholder a $70 dividend with $30 of franking credits. Therefore the $100 is added to the shareholders' income, but at the same time it is registered that $30 has already been paid in tax.
Capital Gains Tax (CGT)	When an asset is sold, there is a CGT event. That means the transaction is liable for CGT. The amount of that taxable gain is declared as income and is taxed at the marginal rate of the payee.
Goods and Services Tax (GST)	GST is a broad based tax of 10% on most goods, services and other items sold or consumed in Australia. The main exception to this is raw food. Another exception, which is a political point at present, is goods bought overseas under the value of $1,000. If you buy goods on the internet under $1,000, there is no GST, but buy the same goods at an Australian retailer and there will be 10% GST. The problem is collecting the tax.

Super Contributions	Concessional contributions are those that are made by your employer or yourself out of your pre-tax income. This is now to a maximum rate of $25,000 per year. Concessional contributions are taxed at 15% instead of your marginal rate.
	Non-concessional contributions are post-tax contributions that you make. These are not taxed going into super, but the earnings are taxed at 15% instead of the marginal rate they would be taxed at if they were invested outside of super.
Super Income	Super income is taxed at 15% in the accumulation phase. That means if you invest in super, your investment earnings will be taxed at 15% instead of your marginal rate.
Land Tax	Start investing in property and you will have to pay land tax. Each state is different, but if you intend to buy an investment property, you need to factor in potential land tax.

6

Business Basics

Most people think the basics of business are managing people, making products or delivering a service, marketing, and production plans. Well, you do need all of that but it comes well after you understand the goals and roles of the various players in the business.

The vast majority of people in business buy themselves a job; they do not plan the business properly or look at it from the point of view of a shareholder or director. This is a top-down analysis of business basics, and without it you are the proverbial rudderless ship.

Financial goals

In relation to financial goals, you have your own business and therefore are in control of your own destiny.

You have short-, medium-, and long-term financial goals.

The short term is how much do you need per week to live. This should come from your salary as an "employee".

The medium is what is required to stabilise lifestyle. This should come from director's fees. You can vary these from year to year.

Long-term is the amount you require in investments to provide enough unearned (investment) income to satisfy your retirement requirements. To get this right, you need to figure out how much capital you will require and what it is invested in and which investment vehicle you are going to use. Never for a minute think that anyone is going to buy your business. The days of "goodwill" are well and truly over. Assets in real estate, equities and cash are all that count. Also, do not think you can pour heaps into super in the last few years; that strategy ends in tears. Therefore, you have to figure out NOW how much you need in 40 years' time, divide it by 40 and start putting that amount away per year. That could be in super contributions, in buying property and getting the business to pay the rent, or in stashing it under the pillow. Just make sure you start now.

Business Roles

Your roles in the financial elements of your life will be a function of your beliefs and your balance. Therefore, it is so important to understand yourself and where you sit in the family of origin, your nuclear family and the community. From a purely financial point of view your main role is the investment of capital. This has three important elements: rate of return, strategy and structure. Your prime objective should be to get the greatest return on the capital available in the long-term. In your business, you have four roles. Those roles must be kept separate and all have defined objectives.

Owner or shareholder

As an owner, you really have only one right and that is to vote at the annual general meeting. At that meeting, you vote in a board which will govern the company.

Director

The board has five major roles:
- To ensure that the company meets all the governing requirements of the entity. (Make sure the company does not break the law.)
- Make sure the company has the funds to pay its current debtors. (Ensure the company is trading solvently.)
- Develop a business plan for the company. Primarily to set aims and objectives for the management to achieve.
- Appoint managerial staff to carry out the plan.
- To audit the financial accounts and present the required

financial reports.

On the board, there are three skill sets required:
- The Entrepreneur. The person with the vision.
- The Administrator. The person that keeps order.
- The Technician. The person that knows how to do the business as outlined in the mission statement.

There must be a balance between these three. One person may take more than one role. Normally the personality required to be an entrepreneur is dissimilar to that required of an administrator. All three must be able to work together otherwise the business model will be skewed in favour of one or another.

Manager

The manager has two basic roles.
1. To set aims and objectives.
2. To coach staff in achieving those aims and objectives.
   Empowering Staff.

You, as the manager, have to make sure the employee has the *integrity* and the *ability* to carry out the job.

Then you have to agree together on
- What the job is. Get them to tell you do not assume they understand.
- Their resources.
- Where their boundaries lie.
- How you are going to measure their performance.

If, as a manager, you are not doing one of these you are not doing your job.

Employee

The role of the employee is to do the tasks set by the manager. It is crucial that you understand the four roles and use each and every one of them.

Financial roles

In a family, you can have many roles. You can be a child, a sibling, a parent, a friend, a cousin, a coach, a mentor or a counsellor. And sometimes you must be all of those at once. At some stages of your life these roles are static and at others they move like sand under your feet.

One of the tough times is when you have an adolescent child. During a day or an hour, you may change from being a parent, to a coach, to a friend, to a disciplinarian, as the adolescent changes from child to adult and back again, in what seems like perpetual motion. The same applies in your financial roles.

Most people focus on their role as a wage earner. In 1980 I was sitting in a real estate agent's office just about to buy a house. His phone rang, he politely asked me if he could answer it. He spoke for about five minutes and then hung up, sat back and sighed. He then explained that the person on the other end of the phone was a 75-year-old woman, who lived on the Gold Coast but owned numerous properties in Hamilton, Brisbane. She was a very wealthy woman.

One day he asked her how she had become wealthy. She answered: "Graham, you are so busy making a living, you will never make any money." I didn't realise it for many years, but that moment changed my financial life. I started to plan my future, to work on the business and not in the business, and I started to segregate my financial roles.

We all have a role as an employee, whether we work for ourselves or others. But currently, for many, there are numerous roles. We all have superannuation funds, whether self-managed, industry, retail, corporate or public sector. For many we are trustees of discretionary trusts, directors of private companies and beneficiaries of trusts.

The number of roles can be too large to comprehend let alone manage. The first step is to understand the individual roles.

In many private companies, a single person finds themselves carrying out all three of these roles. It is important to have goals for each role. It is also important to understand what is required of each role. The prime role for the director is to create the vision. The prime role for the CEO is to use the available capital wisely. The prime role of the employee is to carry out the prescribed duties efficiently.

Now, I know some of you are sitting there thinking, what has this got to do with me? Well, the average Australian wage today is $61,000 per year, and 9.5% of that is $483 per month.

If you invest $480 per month into super for the next 50 years, it will be worth $2.6m at 7%, $3.8m at 8% and $5.6m at 9%. During that time, you will have earned $3m from actually working. Therefore, at 7.5% earnings on your super, you will have earned more than you did working. So, yes, you have a major financial role, and you need to understand it and get the strategy, structure, and return as good as you can.

Discretionary trust roles

Settlor	Starts the trust but has no further involvement.
Appointor	Controls the trust by appointing the trustees.
Trustee	Trustees operate within two sets of formal rules: the governing document which may be called rules or a constitution or the trust deed. The second set of rules are those in the law, particularly the acts which govern their type of organisation. Trustees work collectively as a board and take decisions at formal board meetings. Once a decision has been collectively made, all trustees are bound to support that decision. The trustees hold the assets on behalf of the trust.
Beneficiaries	Receive income distributions from the trust fund as allocated by the trustee. The income received becomes part of the beneficiaries' assessable income and tax is paid at the marginal rate of the beneficiary.

Self-managed superannuation fund roles
1. Trustee
2. Member

Funding

There are numerous levels of funding. All levels are based on the premise of risk and return.

Level 1. The Business angels	These are people that are prepared to fund a business start-up with very high risk and an extreme rate of return. A business angel could give an entrepreneur capital to start a business while looking for a 100% return in the first 12 months.
Level 2. Private Equity	This is when you already have the business but you need money to grow the business. Private equity looks for returns in the order of 20 to 40% per year.
Level 3. Business loan	This is when the business has grown to a point where it has capital behind it and can use that capital to borrow from a bank. The bank requires a mortgage over an asset purchased as their fallback position. Rates vary from 2–6% over the bank rate. Collateral required is around 150% of the amount borrowed. Can require a director's guarantee.
Level 4. Personal loan	This is where you give personal guarantees and use equity of a personal nature, normally your principal place of residence. Here you put everything on the line but the interest rate is reduced.

Business Planning

The business planning process requires a number of steps which are aimed at flushing out the strategic competitive advantages of the business.

Rate of return

It is your responsibility to invest the capital at your disposal to get the highest rate of return possible, within the guidelines of your objectives. Rate of Return is a function of your investment profile and your appetite for risk, which is a function of the timeline in which you are investing.

Strategy

While the rate of return and structure would be classed as mutually exclusive, strategy and structure are interdependent. A structure will be set up with a time frame and a tax structure in mind. The investment strategy must then be aligned with the structure.

Structure

The ultimate value of the assets to the beneficiaries is a function of structure and taxation. There is little point in taking a high-risk position that requires extensive work if it is going to be taxed at the top marginal rate.

Examples: If you set up a discretionary trust to distribute to people with low or little income, you would structure your investments for capital growth. That way the CGT would be paid at the marginal rate of the beneficiary. On the other hand, high-yielding investments would come with franking credits which would be of no use to low income earners. The same would be true of a high-net-worth super fund. You would develop a strategy to pay capital gains in many years to come to avoid the latest 15% income tax. On the other hand, if your super fund is under the

$1.6m limit, you would want as many franking credits as you can get so as to get a refund from the ATO. This may change if the ALP gets it's way. Never forget Newton's third law of motion. In the case of high-net-worth super, funds will structure their investments to provide lower incomes and higher capital gains. This will most likely result in capital moving into areas where capital growth is the norm as opposed to franked income. The result will be a substantial capital movement from Australia to the US.

We have talked about the fact that you will earn more from unearned income in your life than from earned income. The prime role needs to be on the structure into which the capital is placed and the return that is achieved on that capital. You may have roles as a CEO and an employee, but these roles are subservient to your role of the protector and development of your capital. The vast majority of people have no understanding of the accounting process, yet the accounting process gives us the scorecard of our financial endeavours.

Summary

A few of things you need to know about accounting:
1. Over 90% of accountants are financial accountants and are therefore historians.
2. It is only management accounting that will give you the true scorecard.
3. The P&L gives you the historical version of what happened as a function of taxation legislation.
4. The balance sheet is a historical measurement of the capital position and is not the market position.
5. The cash flow analysis is the main indicator of solvency.

You need to understand the goals and roles of the business to drive it. This material will also help you when we get to investing in public corporations. As we will see later, the vast majority of corporations are now outsourcing a lot of these roles and therefore losing a grip on their businesses.

7

Investment basics

Introduction

Every project starts with a need or a problem. Nearly everybody when faced with a problem wants to race in and do something, there is a desperate need to get in and fix it. The problem with that approach is that nine times out of ten the wrong problem gets solved.

When faced with a problem it is important to go about solving it in a rational and precise manner. The following process normally works, limits solving the wrong problem and focuses on getting the best results.

The 10-step problem-solving process

1. Define the problem. More often than not people list a cause as being the problem. Actually defining the problem can be the hardest part of the whole exercise.
2. Quantify the problem. Many people see a problem and put considerable effort into solving the problem only to realise it was not such a big deal after all. It has been found that 80% of problems go away by the time you get here. Lord grant me the courage to change what I can, the humility to know what I can't and the wisdom to know the difference.
3. List all the causes. This is a brainstorming session where you need to drag out all the causes.
4. Categorise the causes.

5. Prioritise the categories. Where will you get the biggest bang for the buck.
6. Draw the vision of what you need to achieve. What does solving the problem look like.
7. Measure where you are. You need a starting point, otherwise you do a whole lot of work and you don't know whether it was worthwhile or not.
8. Create a plan to achieve your objective. How are you going to achieve your aim?
9. Implement the plan. This is where you actually get to do the work.
10. Measure where you have gone. Have you achieved your goal?

Your problem

There are two major parts to the problem.

The first part: There are three stages to your financial life in terms of income.

1. Unearned income. Living off your parents.
2. Earned income when you earn enough to live and meet your financial goals.
3. Unearned income. Where you live off the unearned income you have generated through the earned income phase.

The second part: There are three major expenses in your life. These are expenses that will take more than a year or two to save up for.

4. Your first house. $400,000
5. Educating your children. $300,000 per child.
6. Funding your unearned retirement. $1.2m.

It is up to you to define your problem in detail. These two

parts define your problem. You have a period in the middle of your life where you need to earn and save to build a capital base for your house, education fund and retirement. Each of you will have a different balance and will therefore define a different problem. Some of you will no doubt throw caution to the wind and hope for the best. Good luck with that.

Your problem, in one form or another, is that you will have to earn and save to build the required capital to achieve your objectives. A simple bank account is not going to give you the return required to achieve those objectives, and therefore you will need to invest your savings to gain a return high enough for your needs.

You can invest directly in a property or a house, or you can invest in a managed fund where you put your savings together with others to build a critical mass for investment.

Earlier, we defined investment and gambling; you really need to get a grip on those definitions, because there are so many grey areas between the two.

I have not attempted to list all investments here. This is not an investment manual; it is a description of some of the investments that are available to you. You need to understand the investment environment and then figure out where your strengths lie.

Basically, there are only four types of investment: cash, property, equity, and infrastructure, the new kid on the block.

Once you have figured out what you want to invest in, you have to determine how you are going to make the investment. **The more you do yourself, the less the costs; the more you rely on others the greater the costs.** You have to choose investment styles and strategies, and then you have to structure the investments for your lifelong goal, not for now.

Direct investments
Cash

Cash refers to current assets comprising currency or currency equivalents that can be accessed immediately or near-immediately (as in the case of money market accounts). Currency and coins on hand, bank balances and negotiable bonds.

Notes and coin

Money in coins and notes. Bank accounts. Cash account. Cheque accounts. Savings account.

Fixed interest

Term deposit.

Term deposits are the most familiar type of investments paying interest. They are a savings product from a bank, credit union or building society. Your money is invested for a fixed term and you get a fixed rate of interest over that term.

Bonds

A debt investment in which an investor loans money to an entity (corporate or governmental) that borrows the funds for a defined period at a fixed interest rate.

A bond, also known as a fixed-income security, is a debt instrument created for raising capital. They are essentially loan agreements between the bond issuer and an investor, in which the issuer is obliged to pay amounts of money at future dates.

Hybrids

A single financial security that combines two or more different financial instruments. Hybrid securities, often referred to as "hybrids," generally combine both debt and equity characteristics. The most common type of hybrid security is a convertible bond that has features of an ordinary bond but is heavily influenced by the price movements of the stock into which it is convertible.

Property as in real property

A piece of land or real estate. Property is divided into two types: "real property" which is any interest in land, real estate, growing plants or the improvements on it, and "personal property" (sometimes called "personality") which is everything else.

When buying property, investors are looking for an income and a capital gain. The income comes through rent or a lease, and the capital gain comes from the sale price minus the purchase price. In both cases, there are costs that need to be considered.

Residential

Residential property has always been a popular investment option in Australia. It is an asset class that historically, over the long-term, has produced satisfactory returns for a lot of investors.

Advantages

Low volatility. There is no daily fluctuation of price, making it easier for you to stick with your investment plan.

Taxation. There are considerable tax advantages for residential property. If you hold a property for more than 12 months then the 50% capital gain discount applies when you sell. If you live in your property then generally there is a full capital gains exemption. If you purchase an investment property, there may be tax advantages each year if the property is negatively geared.

Capital growth. Because the bank provides most of the funds for a property purchase, there is considerable leverage and your capital growth returns can be considerable.

Long-term. Investing in property is a long-term wealth creation strategy that can provide investors with consistent returns over the long-term.

Demand. In Australia there appears to be an ongoing housing shortage. National Housing supply council reports indicate that not enough homes are being built by the public and private sectors. This should mean that demand for rental properties should keep rents growing and house prices stable. After all, everyone needs somewhere to live.

Mining. High rental rates can be gained in some areas and as an additional benefit, mining companies often subsidise their employee's rents which should translate to more stability in tenancy and rental return.

- The reverse is also the case, at the end of the mining boom properties in mining towns were reduced in value considerably.

Rent increases. Legislation protecting both the landlord and tenants means that rent increases can be negotiated and need to be reasonable. The Australian government social welfare policies mean that residential property investors can still increase rents where they rent to low income earners because rental assistance through Centrelink is based on market rates.

Disadvantages

Valuation You don't know the exact value of your property unless you want to raise more equity or sell it.

High capital costs Initial capital costs are much greater with property purchases. You need to have available the initial deposit amount for the first property which can be up to 20% of the capital cost.

Liquidity If funds are needed in the short term, property is not an asset that you can quickly liquidate or just sell a small portion.

Costs The costs to buy and sell are quite high for residential property. Stamp duty, mortgage registration and agents costs all need to be considered.

Locality risk   Buying in the wrong location is a real risk for residential property. While other areas are steadily increasing, a wrong location can be stagnant affecting an investor's return over the long-term.

Interest rates   Interest rates play a significant part of the costs of owning a property. When interest rates rise, investors need to be able to bear the brunt of the increased payments.

Negative gearing   If a rental property is negatively geared, then the investor needs to find the difference each month between the income and the expenses.

Property management

Another way in which a smaller investor can make a difference is by taking on the management of a rental property themselves. This option is not for everyone but you may want to consider it for the following reasons: Property management costs can be between 7% and 9% so doing it yourself can save money. (don't forget though that agents' fees are generally tax-deductible) You can ensure that your property is maintained to the standard you want

Valuation

When you start looking for a house you will have access to many real estate agents who will tell you what properties are worth. Their valuation will be based on other sales in the area, the equipment in the house, the state of maintenance and many other issues. While these valuations will give you an insight into what other people think it really has little bearing on what you should be thinking. In fact, the value of a property is what someone else is prepared to pay for it. In this case, that someone may be you.

In simple terms, I believe a house is worth the value of the land and the cost of improvements. That is, you can buy land in the area for so much a square metre and the cost of building that style of building is so much per square metre. That is the value of the house.

It is easy to find out what the land is worth and the cost of building; add them together and you have your valuation. Now we are talking houses so people will say it has to be a nice neighbourhood, it has to be close to nice schools, and so on. These lifestyle values should not be brought into what the house is worth. When you go to sell it, you can assume you will be selling to someone that doesn't care about the same things as you.

Now, when you go to buy it you may decide that you are prepared to pay x above the valuation for the lifestyle properties of the house, but be very clear you need to be prepared to lose that lifestyle value on selling.

Your principal place of residence

The asset value of your home is not included in the asset test. And there is no capital gains tax on your principal place of residence. As a result, the world of the amateur economists has focused on building capital in one's principal place of residence. So let's take a closer look at the investment strategy of the homeowner.

I am going to look at someone on double the average annual earnings at $160,000 per year with a tax bill of $47,000. They are in their first home with a mortgage of $300,000 paying a mortgage at $2,150 per month. Before tax that requires an income of $40,000. That gives you $120,000 per year before tax or $84,000 after tax to live on.

Now this person is still young and hasn't developed any outrageous spending habits, so they say let's upgrade the house. They go and buy a house for $900,000 with borrowings of $800,000. The mortgage goes to $5,740 after tax and $8,200 before tax. If you pay the loan out you will pay $1.375m over 20 years, including $575,547 in interest. During that time, you will have paid about $420,000 in tax on your earnings. So in before-tax dollars, you have paid $1.8m for the house to avoid paying CGT on the sale.

But wait, there is more. All the rates, electricity, maintenance and improvement costs are out of after-tax dollars. It constantly amazes me that supposedly intelligent people can convince themselves that living in an upgraded house is a good investment decision.

The fact is that Robert Kiyosaki is dead right; your principal place of residence is, in fact, probably the greatest liability you will even own. The average residential real estate property returns about 2% after taking costs into account. If you add the cost of income tax into the equation, most people lose on their residential properties, but few are prepared to do the maths. If you want a big, expensive house that is fine, but put it under the title of cost of lifestyle do not try to convince yourself it is a good investment.

Commercial

Real estate that is used for business activities. Commercial properties fall into many categories, including industrial properties, shopping centres, farms, offices or even vacant land.

When you make an investment, you want an overall return which is made up of income and capital growth. The first thing you need is capital growth to at least the level of the Consumer Price index (CPI), then you want some capital growth on top of that and then you need income.

Most investors want an overall return of about 10%; this lines up with what you can get with equities. Commercial property is sold on the value of the lease. Valuations are generally a function of the potential earnings into the future. Therefore, if a property has a lease that returns 6% on the asking price, it would be a good deal if you considered that a 4% capital growth was achievable.

Pricing changes as the market cycles change. In a high interest rate environment, the returns will have to be high and therefore the capital growth will be lower. However, when interest rates are low people expect that capital will grow quickly and therefore they are prepared to except a lower income return.

A very important part of commercial real estate is the transactional costs. These can be very substantial. In most cases, you are not buying the property outright, you will be getting finance from a bank or other lending institution. The bank will require more paperwork and many legal documents. It is not abnormal for the transactional costs to end up costing the equivalent of one year's income. Therefore, it is important to take those costs into account when developing the business plan around the purchase.

Costs associated with property investments
1. Purchase fees
    - Real estate agents
    - Legal fees
    - Permits
    - Borrowing costs
    - Stamp duty
2. Maintenance fees
    - Council rates
    - Insurance.
    - Body corporate
    - Maintenance
    - Land tax
3. Selling costs
    - Real estate agents
    - Stamp duty
    - Legal fees
    - Engineering reports

- Environmental reports
- Capital gains tax
- Financial advice
- Management fees

Conclusion

For most people, property tends to be a more emotional investment than equities, and as a result there is a tendency to fudge the figures by leaving out expenses or taxes in the final analysis. It is true that if you had bought property at any time in history, it would nearly always have increased in value, but it is easy to leave out the costs of holding such an investment.

On the other hand, property is something you can see and touch, unlike the projected future returns of a digitally based corporation that holds few assets.

REITs: Real estate investment trusts

A security that sells like a stock on the major exchanges and invests in real estate directly, either through properties or mortgages. Real-estate investment trusts (REITs) receive special tax considerations and typically offer investors high yields, as well as a highly liquid method of investing in real estate.

Equities

A stock or any other security representing an ownership interest. An equity investment generally refers to the buying and holding of shares of stock on a stock market by individuals and firms in anticipation of income from dividends and capital gains, as the value of the stock rises.

When buying equities an investor is looking for a capital gain and an income, as they are in property. The size of each of these will depend on the circumstances of the individual investor.

Over the last 100 years the average of the top 200 stocks on the Australian market has delivered an 11% return per year. This is normally around 6% income and 5% capital gain.

The US market differs in that many American equities pay no dividends, that is there is no income. To obtain an income from your investment you need to progressively sell your shares.

This difference is driven by the tax structures in the two economies.

Shares

A unit of ownership in a corporation or financial asset. While owning shares in a business does not mean that the shareholder has direct control over the business's day-to-day operations, being a shareholder does entitle the possessor to an equal distribution in any profits, if any are declared in the form of dividends. The two main types of shares are common shares and preferred shares.

In Australia, we have what are called franked dividends. The company in which you own shares makes a profit and pays tax on that profit. Instead of the shareholder then being taxed again on the profit, known as double taxation, the company pays the dividend with franking credits which represent the tax already paid. When looking at your return it is important to take the franking credits into account.

Valuation of equities

There are many ways you can value an equity. Of course, the true value is what someone is prepared to pay for it. Therefore, the value on the stock market is the true value of the equity. Well, yes and no.

There are three primary equity value models:

Discounted cash flow (DCF). DCF analysis uses future free cash flow projections and discounts to arrive at a present value estimate. I am not even going to try to spin the maths here, you will have to do the research for yourself. The basic premise is that the company is worth the value of its future earnings discounted for the time value of money and the risk. There are many variations on this. I had one accountant who valued a company on the risk value of the last year's earnings, and another that made the same valuation based on the last three years.

Cost   This is really a balance sheet approach and is relevant in some cases.

Comparable   This is comparing the company you are looking at against other similar companies.

The important issue is that valuation is as much an art as it is a science. It used to be a good rule of thumb that you thought of yourself as buying a future income stream, however in today's market it is easy to see that income could change overnight if there is a disruptive competitor on your heels.

The old method was to look at future earnings, but these days they are not assured. You could also look at the balance sheet of the potential purchase, but these days that means nothing. Apple has a market value of US$754 billion but its actual operating assets account for only 5% of that value. Think about what that means. If someone out-Apples Apple, then it is worthless. The same applies to Amazon: a US$450 billion company that has operating assets more in line with Apple than BHP.

The point I am trying to make is that the equities market used to be used for investors to buy a future income stream, they would hold that investment until they had news that something was likely to upset that income stream. Today the equity market, along with the currency markets and the futures market are much closer to a trading market than an investment market. Traders use the equity market to try to find an edge. Most equities are traded to make a trading profit rather than relying on the company to make a profit for them.

Rights issues

A rights issue is when a company issues its existing shareholders a right to buy additional shares in the company. It will offer the shareholder a specific number of shares at a specific price. The company will also set a time limit for the shareholder. The shares are often offered at a discounted price to encourage existing shareholders to take the company up on their offer. If a shareholder does not take the company up on their rights issue, they have the option to sell their rights on the stock market just as they would sell ordinary shares, but their shareholding in the company will weaken.

Share purchase plans

An investment service that allows individuals to purchase a stock directly from a company or through a transfer agent. Not all companies offer DSPPs and the plans often have restrictions on when an individual can purchase shares.

Costs associated with equity transactions

a) Purchase
    1. Brokerage
    2. GST

b) Sale
    1. Brokerage
    2. GST
    3. CGT

c) Financial advice

d) Financial management

When you add up all the players and all the costs, it is self-evident that the purpose of the market is for secondary trading and not for the allocation of assets. The system started off as a simple mechanism whereby a single investor could buy equity in a company. However, the financial sector has turned that on its head and turned the market into a side show for the major secondary market.

It started with churning. This is when your broker tells you that banks are the place to invest, and at the moment the ANZ is the best buy on the market. You buy the ANZ shares. In the next reporting period, the broker tells you the ANZ is on the nose and you need to buy CBA. This goes on and on and you stay in the bank market but change from bank to bank. In the meantime, your broker picks up brokerage, and your adviser picks up fees.

Hedge fund

Hedge funds aim to create value through their manager's skill and do not rely solely on market growth to make profits. They have the flexibility to use derivatives and arbitrage strategies and may offer performance potential and diversification benefits. Hedge funds are like managed funds in that investments are pooled and professionally managed, but differ in that the fund has far more flexibility in its investment strategies. The general objective of a hedge or absolute return fund is to provide investors with positive returns in most market conditions. Many hedge fund managers also invest a significant proportion of their own wealth into the funds they manage.

ETFs: Exchange Traded Funds

An ETF, or exchange traded fund, is a marketable security that tracks an index, a commodity, bonds or a basket of assets like an index fund. It trades close to its NTA at all times.

ETFs are a simple way to create a diversified portfolio. They are traded on the Australian Stock Exchange in the same way as shares. An ETF generally invests in a basket of shares that makes up an index, and there are an increasing number of ETFs to choose from. You can also choose to invest in ETFs over currency or commodities.

As we make our way through the environment in which we live we relate to the history of that environment. In the case of equities there were only a very small number of people that purchased equities up until the 1960s. Remember that over 90% of the world's population lived in poverty in the early 1900s.

It was after the second world war that a middle class started to grow. The majority in that middle class spent their money on bigger homes and flash cars, but a select few started to save for their retirement. The main vehicle was life insurance and insurance bonds. However, legislative changes and sophistication of the market saw a change from insurance companies to other financial institutions. In the 1970s, even cab drivers started to buy shares.

In many ways share trading was a bit like going to the casino. A lack of transparency ensured that insiders had a much better chance of reading the market. As a result, there was a massive growth of stockbroking houses and managed-fund operators. A huge industry grew up around the purchasing of equities. As the market and the processes got more and more sophisticated the number of people in the supply chain increased until the average return to the client was about 4% less than the real return of the investments. The fee gouging in the industry has grown to a crescendo. Those that are in the market have been wise to it for a decade.

Later we will discuss active versus passive portfolio management. But here we take the point that active management incurs fees that are greater than the increased returns. In 2007 Warren Buffett made a bet that the index would outdo the hedge funds over a 10-year period. The next year the market dropped 37% and it looked like Buffett was going to lose. But Buffett won the bet by a country mile.

For the last decade including the global financial crisis (GFC), the market index funds have done substantially better than the actively managed hedge funds. What amateur investor would even think of picking stocks?

The major driving force behind ETFs has been their performance, though of later times there has been another major factor, and that has been the FOFA (Future of Financial Advice) legislation, which was passed on June 25th 2012 and took effect on July 1st 2012. FOFA basically says that any financial adviser has to act in the best interests of their clients. That can cause a lot of issues when a recommended stock goes south. Therefore, a good bet is a bet on an index, in line with the risk profile of the investor, and it keeps the financial adviser out of jail. How good is that—getting paid for putting investors into index funds? Still, that is much better then losing 4% on fees in the whole of the supply chain.

Listed Investment Companies (LICs)

LICs are a viable and well established alternative to the managed fund and in fact have some considerable advantages when compared to managed funds. LICs are a great way to achieve market diversification or invest conservatively for those investors without the expertise or inclination to invest directly in other ASX listed companies.

Structure

Most LICs are companies that usually distribute their income by way of fully franked dividends on which 30% (company) tax is already paid.

Asset exposure

You can choose an LIC that suits your investment needs from the following profiles.

Domestic Focus.
    Large Cap.
    Large to Medium Cap.

Medium to Small Cap.
   Small Cap.
   Long/Short.
   Market Neutral.
   Enhanced Income.
International Focus
   Global
   Asian
And other specialist areas.

Net tangible assets (NTA)

The value of the underlying assets held by an LIC on a per-share basis is referred to as NTA (net tangible assets). LICs are required to report their NTA on a regular basis and this measure can be used to determine whether an LIC is trading at a premium or a discount to its NTA.

Current and historical LIC premiums/discounts to NTA data is available from the ASX site and can be used to help investors time their buying and selling. Closed-end LICs do not regularly issue new shares or cancel shares as investors join and leave the fund. Investors buy and sell shares in LICs from each other through the stock exchange. This allows an LIC to concentrate on investment selection without having to factor in the possibility of money leaving the fund unexpectedly as in the case of a managed fund.

Costs

Generally, a long-established LIC charges a management expense ratio (MER) significantly below comparably invested unlisted managed funds. Usually this is a result of long-term buy and hold strategies which cost less, and usually LICs are internally managed, which results in lower costs.

In recent years there has been an explosion in the number of Listed Investment Companies. They have expanded in geographic and industry areas of exposure. They are also splitting into two sections. The first is the standard LIC which has been around for nearly 100 years were the MER is less than 1% in fact down to less than 0.2%. And now there is the new model which has fees over 1% and also high performance fees. I refer to these as LICKS.

Transparency

LICs must comply with the stock exchange's corporate governance and reporting requirements, which means that they are generally more transparent than a managed fund.

Liquidity

Most LICs are traded easily on the ASX, but some LICs can be quite thinly traded.

Volatility

LICs are prone to the overall volatility of the stock market and this may be a disadvantage to some investors.

Regular savings

Unlike a managed fund, LICs don't offer a regular savings program, which means an investor will need to accumulate funds over a period of time to invest in a meaningfully sized parcel. One way would be to set up an online broking account and deposit your regular savings to the attached high-yielding savings account. Every quarter or other regular interval perhaps, buy as many shares of the LIC as possible with the available balance.

Equities versus real estate

The big question has always been which is the best investment: real estate or equities? Like all things in life it is not that simple. What sort of real estate and what equities are we looking at. The other parameter is the investor themselves. You need to judge your skill level and figure out where you can add the most value. In real estate if you buy an investment property and use contractors to rent it, manage it and maintain it, your profit can go up in fees. On the equity side if you pay a financial adviser, fund manager and fund of fund manager, your profits will disappear in fees. So, what are your skills and how much are you prepared to do.

The other thing is that you have to compare apples with apples, and that is very difficult to achieve.

In equities if you look at the All Ords over the last 30 years, you would have returned 9.1% per year, year after year. That includes reinvesting dividends, but doesn't include the value of the franking credits. So, many would say the All Ords has returned 11.5% per year over the last 30 years.

In residential housing the capital market has increased by about 9% per year over the last 30 years, on top of that after expenses you would expect to get an income of about 2% meaning the total return would be 11%. So that's easy, they are about the same. However, that is not all true.

During the 30 years, the shares in the All Ordinaries have changed and you'll have had to trade in line with those changes, or you might have invested in an LIC or managed fund which tracked the index and that may have performed better or worse than the index. ETFs weren't around 30 years ago.

In real estate, the average house was very different 30 years ago to what it is now. It has increased in size, got more mod cons (toys to play with), and is built to a better standard. If you bought a house 30 years ago it would not have increased its value at the rate of 9% per year.

What you invest in is up to you. You cannot be skilled in all fields; you need to make a choice, especially in the beginning.

Derivatives

A derivative is a security whose price is dependent upon or derived from one or more underlying assets. The derivative itself is merely a contract between two or more parties. Its value is determined by fluctuations in the underlying asset. The most common underlying assets include stocks, bonds, commodities, currencies, interest rates and market indexes. Most derivatives are characterised by high leverage.

Option. A contract that allows the holder to buy or sell an underlying security at a given price, known as the strike price. The two most common types of options contracts are put and call options, which give the holder-buyer the right to sell or buy respectively, the underlying at the strike if the price of the underlying crosses the strike. Typically, each options contract is written on 100 shares of the underlying.

Warrant. A derivative security that gives the holder the right to purchase securities (usually equity) from the issuer at a specific price within a certain time frame. Warrants are often included in a new debt issue as a "sweetener" to entice investors.

Contract-for-difference (CFD). An arrangement made in a futures contract whereby differences in settlement are made through cash payments, rather than the delivery of physical goods or securities.

Infrastructure

Is the basic physical and organisational structures and facilities needed for the operation of a society or enterprise. This means roads, buildings, powerlines, dams, rail, pipes and much more.

As discussed, in politics the socialists believe that this infrastructure should be built, owned and operated by the government. Whereas the capitalists believe it is more efficient in the hands of the private sector. What has happened in Australia in the last 100 years is that a lot of the infrastructure built by government has been sold off to the private sector these include Commonwealth Bank of Australia, Telstra, Qantas and many power stations and transmission lines. Infrastructure has been added as an asset class over the last few years. You can now invest in airports, tunnels, water, ports, communications, energy, toll roads and gas distribution. The process is that the infrastructure is normally built by a developer who then leases it to an operator for a long period, 10 to 30 years. So, in effect, you are buying an income stream. Do not expect big capital gains but do expect a steady stream of dividends which should outperform bonds or cash deposits.

Transparency

Governance was a subject discussed in detail earlier on, and at the time it was clear that you cannot regulate or legislate against bad behaviour. We now have greater prudential control than ever before yet we still manage to live in a world where insider trading, fraud and plain theft are rife. There are so many opportunities for information to get to investors. We have those that are in the in-crowd and lunch with people that have information, we have others that are in the pipeline of information and we have decision makers that either meet in the Qantas Lounge, chairman's of course, who are in the know. It is impossible for the private investor to have any inkling of what is going on in most listed companies. The balance sheets and P&Ls that are provided in annual reports tell you almost nothing and come out months too late to be of any real interest in many decisions.

It is simply not possible for a single investor to gain enough information to make a good investment decision. That means that you have to find a way to get the best out of the market without actually being directly in it.

Managed Investments

The biggest problem you have when starting out is to have enough funds to make the investment you want. Some investments with lower fees require minimum investments of hundreds of thousands of dollars. A way around the problem is to pool your resources with a lot of other people.

A managed fund is a way for you to invest money alongside others, hopefully, to get some benefits by being in a group, as opposed to making your investment directly. The way a managed fund works is that you buy 'units' in the fund directly from the fund manager and, at some point in the future, sell these units back to that same manager. The value of units is re-calculated on a regular basis as the market value of the assets in the fund rise and fall.

Managed investments are sometimes called collective investments or pooled investments. They are known by a number of different names including investment funds, managed funds, unit trusts and managed products.

Buying units in a managed fund has a number of advantages including the fact that the investments are being made by professional managers with access to a large capital base, which means they can access a much more diversified portfolio both locally and internationally. There is also an easy exit because of the liquidity.

On the other hand, there are a number of disadvantages including the costs and fees, the fact that you lose control of the actual investments, and that the manager may make decisions that are contrary to your taxation considerations.

Investment management

Investment management is the professional asset management of various securities (shares, bonds and other securities) and other assets (eg, real estate) to meet specified investment goals for the benefit of the investors. Investors may be institutions (insurance companies, pension funds, corporations, charities, educational establishments etc.) or private investors (both directly via investment contracts and more commonly via collective investment schemes eg, mutual funds or exchange-traded funds).

The term asset management is often used to refer to the investment management of collective investments, while the more generic fund management may refer to all forms of institutional investment as well as investment management for private investors. Investment managers who specialise in advisory or discretionary management on behalf of (normally wealthy) private investors may often refer to their services as money management or portfolio management often within the context of so-called "private banking".

The provision of investment management services includes elements of financial statement analysis, asset selection, stock selection, plan implementation and ongoing monitoring of investments. Coming under the remit of financial services, many of the world's largest companies are at least in part investment managers and employ millions of staff.

Theories of investment management
Active management

Active management involves a single manager, co-managers, or a team of managers who attempt to beat the market return by actively managing a fund's portfolio through investment decisions based on research and decisions on individual holdings. Closed-end funds are generally actively managed.

Hedge funds

Hedge funds have attracted growing investor interest in Australia, particularly in recent years, when the returns from traditional equity investments have, with the exception of the past year, been relatively poor. There is no standard definition of a hedge fund; the name is typically applied to managed funds that use a wider range of financial instruments and investment strategies than traditional managed funds, including the use of short selling and derivatives to create leverage, with the aim of generating positive returns regardless of overall market performance.

This implies that hedge funds are active managed funds on steroids. You read above the story of Warren Buffet and the hedge fund bet.

The massive fees are not the only downside of the hedge funds.

Passive management

Passive management simply tracks a market index, commonly referred to as indexing or index investing.

Absolute return

The return that an asset achieves over a certain period of time. This measure looks at the appreciation or depreciation (expressed as a percentage) that an asset—usually a stock or a mutual fund—achieves over a given period.

Absolute return differs from relative return because it is concerned with the return of an asset and does not compare it to any other measure or benchmark.

Conviction management

High-conviction portfolios contain holdings of securities that an investment manager believes will have the highest expected return, in essence their best ideas. As a result, high-conviction portfolios are expected to generate a higher level of return than a manager's standard portfolio. A high-conviction portfolio typically comprises large holdings of a relatively small number of stocks. An investment manager will therefore pay little attention to country, industry and stock weighting relative to an index benchmark when constructing this type of portfolio. As a result, the expected risk or volatility of the portfolio is also higher.

Value adding

Financial planners, investment managers, portfolio managers and fund managers all play a role in the investment chain. Each one takes a management fee. There can be up to six or seven fee takers in the chain. You often hear about private equity funds returning up to 25%, however by the time it gets down to the retail investor the return can be as low as 7–8%.

Each manager in the chain has to add more value than they take out in fees. Therefore, you need to be able to measure the value that each member in the chain adds.

The main LICs have returned 11–11.5% to their shareholders over the last 20 years. They work on management fees of 0.1–1.2%. If we take 11% as the baseline, that means that if you appoint a financial adviser that charges 1%, and he appoints a fund manager who charges another 1%, then between them they need to invest in funds or companies that return around 13%. The longer the chain gets the harder it is to make it work for you. On the other side the longer the chain and the higher return required the greatest will be the risk in the investment. And logic will tell you that the higher the risk the greater the chance of a negative result.

Diversification

Many would say you need to diversify into a number of investment categories as well as within a single category. Obviously, size helps with diversification, as it allows you to access a wider variety of investments. Diversification means buying for capital growth as well as defensive investments so that you do not make as much in the good times but do not lose as much in the downturns. However, there is another train of thought and that is the one championed by Warren Buffett, so you need to think carefully about it. That thought is that you buy good companies and hang on to them for the long-term. If you have done your homework well you will beat the market.

You need to be aware of diversity across many parameters and also within those parameters.

Investment category

Cash	Term deposits Bonds Hybrids
Shares	Industry Managers Options

Property	o Residential
	    Unit, Duplex, House
	o Commercial
	    Retail, Wholesale, Industrial
	o Rural
	    Agricultural, Lifestyle

Portfolio Management

The art and science of making decisions about investment mix and policy, matching investments to objectives, asset allocation for individuals and institutions, and balancing risk against performance. Portfolio planning is all about strengths, weaknesses, opportunities and threats in the choice of debt vs. equity, domestic vs. international, growth vs. safety, and many other trade-offs encountered in the attempt to maximise return at a given appetite for risk.

Portfolio planning is normally handled by a financial adviser or financial planner, whose job is to personally coach you in what to do with your money. They bring the right knowledge, expertise and guidance to identify and help you achieve your specific lifestyle goals. It means you'll also be partnered with a qualified professional who's committed to helping you realise your financial possibilities.

Using the information you've given them, your financial planner will look at the seven key building blocks (or strategies) of creating wealth. These include:

1. Budgeting
2. Investing
3. Managing debt
4. Managing tax
5. Super
6. Protection
7. Social security

A financial planner charges anywhere between $2,000 to $5,000 for a first interview and then commonly about 1.5–2.0% of your net wealth per year as an ongoing management fee.

However, with FOFA this is getting a lot better. You can have a one-off fee for an SOA (a statement of advice) and then renegotiate a yearly fee afterwards. Do not forget 1% extra over your working life in super means $1m at retirement.

Borrowing basics: loans

To invest, especially in large assets like property, you will more than likely have to borrow funds. Borrowing to invest in a share portfolio can also be a sound strategy. Often, borrowing to invest is considered a risky venture, but we all generally have to borrow to make our biggest investment, the one in our own home, so it is simply a matter of applying similar principles when we borrow to invest.

Home loans

You can apply for a home loan with any number of financial institutions but make sure you do your research on where to get the best package and rate available. Alternatively, you could use the services of a mortgage broker to help you explore your home loan options.

Investment loans

A good investment loan can make the process of purchasing a property for investment purposes straightforward and easy to manage during the life of your investment. Investment loans can vary in complexity and what you choose will depend on what you are trying to achieve.

Types of investment loans

Principal and interest

The simplest of loans and usually used by owner occupiers who are paying the loan with the intention of eventually owning the property. Every regular payment pays off interest and a proportion of the principal borrowed.

Interest only

Usually the preference of loan types for investors who only want to pay off the interest which is generally tax-deductible (principal repayments are not deductible). You can usually request an interest only period from 1 to 5 years and often banks will allow this period to be renegotiated.

Line of credit

You can access the equity in a property by securing a line of credit against that property. A Line of credit loan can be drawn upon, paid down and redrawn numerous times for different purposes. Keeping track of the purpose of the loan drawings is important for investors when considering the tax deductibility of interest repayments, but they are useful if the loan is not fully drawn down so that there is a buffer available to cover any shortfalls in rental payments over the term of the investment. They are also useful to have pre-approved so that you have the funds available to purchase your next property investment.

Other options

Other types of loans can include loans with redraw facilities (note that you should only use redrawn funds for investment purposes), loans with a 100% offset account attached (useful to save paying tax on savings while reducing interest paid on the loan), split loans (useful if you want to take advantage of low interest rates to fix while at the same time having the flexibility to redraw or offset on the variable component).

Margin loan

Margin lending is an investment strategy that lets you borrow money to invest. The assets you buy with the borrowed money are used as security for the loan.

Reverse Mortgage

Reverse Mortgages are loans that allow home owners to borrow money using the equity in a home as security to help cover essential expenses such as home repairs or maintenance or even for personal use such as a new car or holiday.

Investment objectives

Each individual investor will have a different objective, and that objective will change over time. An objective is like a goal. You need to set realistic objectives that are going to stretch you to reach, but are not so high that you are never going to make them.

The principal objectives are as follows.

Preservation of capital

Investment is the process of investing money for profit. The money that you invest is your capital, therefore it is of prime importance that you hang on to your capital. Yes, you can also borrow more against the capital and then leverage your capital. That all makes sense but it all goes to hell in a hand basket if you have no capital.

Breaking up the family trust, for example, would mean breaking up the family's capital, and that is something you cannot afford to do. If you do, you get wiped from the board and have to start all over again.

We will go through this in detail when discussing intergenerational wealth, but the point needs to be made at this stage of the process that your prime objective must be to grow your capital base. Capital leads to income and capital growth. Without capital, you are at the bottom of the heap.

Current income

This whole process is about balance. It is great to have investment plans but you also have to live in the present. What income do you need now to feel comfortable? Defining your current income is a function of budgeting and as your family grows that becomes a function of your relationships. You cannot do this alone; a key driver of the investment plan is your budget and that has to be something that you agree upon with all the stakeholders.

Purchase a home

What type of home? What standard of home? There is a great debate going on in Australia in 2018 about the affordability of housing. The price of housing has gone up dramatically in certain areas however in others it is more than affordable. The word balance comes to mind.

Educate children

Different schools suit different children. The best school for one child may not be the best for another. The cost of education should be looked at as a whole, and not just the simple cost of a school.

Retirement living

A great misnomer is that you can live comfortably on 75% of your final income. You have to evaluate what your retirement looks like, budget for it and then figure out how much you need to achieve your objectives.

Holidays

Holidays used to be about having a break from work. They seem to have become about a whole range of activities that do not relate to recharging batteries.

Toys

Some toys relate to kudos, some relate to lifestyle and some relate to dreams. While you want to have toys to play with now, you do not want to raise the bar too high for the future.

Being in the boating world I see people spending a fortune on toys they just do not have the time to play with. Get the balance right.

Investment strategies

Investments will be driven by the investment objectives, but there are a number of strategies that can drive the plan towards those objectives.

"Top-down" takes a macro look at the general economic circumstances, the politics and cyclical factors.

"Bottom-up" looks at the micro issues of the company itself including the management, the place in the market and the opportunities presented.

Value investing

Companies are valued for any number of reasons. Given that the market is driven by fear and greed, it is often the case that stocks are devalued for emotional reasons and present to the investor a great value opportunity. If you look at the management, the environment and the opportunities you will find stocks trading at a discount to their long-term value.

Buy and hold is a subset of this strategy. Obviously, you invest in companies with value, but as time goes on those companies can lose their value and you need to move on. Some would say that long-term value-based strategies invariably morph into set and forget strategies. The balance is between keeping your eye on value stocks and churning for the sake of churning.

Growth investing

A growth investor looks at a stock with a view to future earnings. It has been said many times the value of a stock is the value of its future earnings. When the investor believes that a company will have an increase in earnings over the investment period, then they will buy the equity on the basis that it will grow in price as those future earnings become a reality.

Technical analysis

This is the use of computer models to foresee the future based on the past. It is also known as charting. "What goes up comes down." "History repeats itself." There are many ways of saying that we live in a cyclical world. The technical analyst uses this cyclical world to predict the future.

Contrarian investing

This is about buying the unpopular equities. When everybody else is selling, you buy. It is known that the market is driven by fear and greed. When fear takes over you buy, when greed takes over you sell.

Thematic investing

This is a subset of top-down investing. You pick a theme and run with it.

These five strategies are not mutually exclusive, they do cross over. Once you discover a theme you will want to pick a value stock within that theme. The strategies are a guide to stop knee jerk reactions and emotional decisions. They also let you make decisions on the run as your moves can be pre-planned.

Investment plan

You need an objective, then you need a strategy and a plan to get there. The following is a six step plan with proven results over many decades.

1. Maintain enough cash to give you stability and security. Make sure you have enough cash to be able to use in opportunities or unknown setbacks.
2. Invest on a monthly basis. Firstly, you need to commit to saving a certain amount each month, and then you need to invest that amount every month.
3. Buy quality; do not go for the impulsive or the big bet. Build a solid base of quality stocks, preferably paying consistent dividends.
4. Take a long-term or objective orientated view. Do not react to short-term market fluctuations.
5. Continue to educate yourself and your family. Earn more than you spend and build a solid future.
6. Set the plan in place, monitor where it is going and review it against your goals.

Risk management

Everyone in the financial chain looks at its risk profile. In general, the greater the risk, the greater the rewards. Investors require a greater return on their funds as the risk increases. So how do you measure risk? Risk is the potential of losing something of value.

We are making a plan that is going to last 60 years and more. During that time, there are going to be any number of events that may cause you to lose something of value. Some of those events will be small and you will soon forget the loss. Others may be catastrophic to your plan. You have potential risk of life and limb or of property. Insurance is a way of sharing that risk with someone else. In fact, with many other people. You pay an amount of money to the insurance company and they collect similar amounts from many other people. If the thing you insured against happens the other people will pay for your misfortune.

I think this is where society gets it wrong in relation to national events. When there is a public catastrophe people demand payment from the government. In fact, they are demanding money from other taxpayers for their misfortune.

You can also insure against damage you may cause to other people or things. This is called liability insurance. Obviously the more you insure the higher the cost. We are in another balancing situation.

I have to say that when I was in business the day the insurance people came was probably the worst day of the year. They are just so depressing. You go through the insurances line by line and each year they dream up more things you need to be insured against. You really have to be aware of your risk profile and your overall plan. It is easy to get sold more insurance than you need; on the other hand, you need to make sure that if you do lose something of value, that you either have it insured or you know you can live without it.

The next issue after what to insure is for how much. Saving a few dollars on premiums can be a really poor decision.

The bottom line is that insurance is a risk-management tool.

There are two major types of insurance.

General insurance

General insurance provides financial protection against loss or damage to property and other assets. General insurance also encompasses liability insurance, consumer credit protection, and personal sickness and accident insurance. With insurance, you need to be especially careful with the documentation. Insurance companies are famous for collecting premiums and then finding a reason not to pay you when you make a claim.

Be careful of the definitions they use. The policy will include the amount covered, location details, optional components, special restrictions, excess levels, the premium and present or potential discounts.

Do not be in a hurry to sign a contract if you do not understand it or you need more time. The insurance company will extend to you the option of a cover note, which is effectively temporary insurance while you get the detail correct.

There should also be a cooling off period. If you find out that the product is not what you want, normally within 14 days you can cancel it and get your premium repaid to you pro rata.

Life insurance

There are many sayings in life like, "It never rains, it pours". As an invincible teenager, you have no idea what that means, however as a parent with a mortgage it can become horribly clear in a short space of time. Remember it is not the balance sheet or even the P&L that will bring you undone; it is cash flow. When you have a young family with a big mortgage, cash flow is incredibly important. If anything should happen to you it can bring your house crumbling down around you.

A lot of people think about life insurance but disability can be a lot worse financially. You do not want to be so risk averse you cannot afford to pay the mortgage, but you need to have a plan in the case of accident, illness, or disability.

The old policies of whole of life and endowment insurance have been replaced by term life, total and permanent disablement (TPD) and trauma insurance. Whereas the old life insurances had an investment component the new policies are a straight risk-management policy.

Term life insurance pays a lump sum benefit upon the death of the life insured.

TPD policies are generally paid as a lump sum. There are two major types "own occupation" and "any occupation".

There are many tricks in the life insurance business. Many can be financially devastating. A work colleague's son was killed in a boating accident. His life was insured in his name. The insurance company would therefore only pay the lump sum to the person who had died. The result was the payment was made to the estate six months after his death. The widow then had to wait for probate. It was lucky that the body had been found, because if it wasn't then the widow would have had to wait 7 years for a death certificate.

If you have own occupation TPD, which for tax reasons is held in your superannuation fund, then the benefit is paid to the superannuation fund and may not be able to be paid out to the member until the member is classified as having a permanent incapacity therefore fulfilling a condition of release under the *Superannuation Industry Act 1993*.

The purpose of TPD insurance is to provide a benefit where the life insured suffers an illness or injury and is unable to ever work again.

Trauma insurance is used to provide the life insured with a lump sum so they can have financial access to medical care, rehabilitation and lifestyle changes.

TPD premiums can be a tax deduction, while trauma insurance premiums are generally not tax-deductible.

Income protection insurance pays an instalment benefit if the life insured, because of a sickness or injury, is unable to work in their own occupation. You can have an income-protection policy (IPP) on an agreed value or indemnity value basis.

Business overheads insurance

Business overheads insurance is for someone who owns their own business and is forced to stop work because of sickness or injury. While the revenue they generate may stop, the expenses keep rolling on in.

There are three types of business expenses insurance policies. Indemnity, reimbursement and agreed value.

There are also business uses of life insurance including key person insurance, business liability insurance, buy–sell insurance and business overhead insurance.

Some insurances can be purchased through superannuation funds and some cannot. Some are a tax deduction and some are not.

The point is that this is a very complex matter, you may never need it but if something does happen you may be in big trouble without it. Like everything in our world, the rules are changing all the time and the complexity increases. Get yourself a good adviser and do a lot of research yourself. Do not wait until it is too late. The last thing you need if there is illness or injury is to be worrying about financial issues.

Net return

Earnings

Anything that is income as a result of the investment. They come in the form of interest, dividends, rent, coupons and any other income generated.

Expenses

These are the costs of developing the strategy, planning the investments, placing the investments, managing the investments. They come in the form of fees and charges.

Tax

Must be taken into account before you can arrive at your net return. Tax is a function of structure and the entity used for the investment. Tax is also an important part of the investment structure and management of the fund.

Examples of taxes: income tax, stamp duty, company tax, land tax.

Legal entities

A legal entity is an individual, company or organisation that has legal rights and obligations.

Individual

In a legal sense a natural person is a person that is an individual human being, as opposed to a legal person, which may be a private or public organisation.

Sole trader

A person who is the exclusive owner of a business is entitled to keep all profits after tax has been paid but is liable for all losses.

The following is from the ATO.

A sole trader is an individual running a business. It is the simplest and cheapest business structure.

If you operate your business as a sole trader, you are the only owner and you control and manage the business.

You are legally responsible for all aspects of the business. Debts and losses can't be shared with other individuals.

You can employ workers in your business, but you can't employ yourself.

As a sole trader, you are responsible for paying your workers' super. You're also responsible for your own super and may choose to pay it into a fund for yourself to help save for your retirement.

Key features

As a sole trader, you use your individual tax file number when lodging your income tax return report all your income in your individual tax return, using the section for business items to show your business income and expenses (there is no separate business tax return for sole traders) apply for an ABN and use your ABN for all your business dealings register for goods and services tax (GST) if your annual GST turnover is $75,000 or more pay tax at the same income tax rates as individual taxpayers and you may be eligible for the small business tax offset put aside money to pay your income tax at the end of the financial year – usually, you will do this by paying quarterly Pay As You Go (PAYG) instalments claim a deduction for any personal super contributions you make after notifying your fund. As a sole trader, you can't claim deductions for money 'drawn' from the business. Amounts taken from the business are not wages for tax purposes, even if you think of them as wages.

Personal services income (PSI)

If you're paid mostly for your personal efforts, skills or expertise, you might be receiving personal services income (PSI) and you may have to treat deductions in relation to this income differently.

Partnership

A partnership is not a separate legal entity. Each partner is fully responsible for debts and liabilities incurred by the other partners—with or without their knowledge.

A partnership is an arrangement in which two or more individuals share the profits and liabilities of a business venture. Various arrangements are possible: all partners might share liabilities and profits equally, or some partners may have limited liability.

The advantage of a partnership used to be that, like a discretionary trust, the profits go straight to the partners who add the profits to their own tax income, without the partnership paying tax as a company would. However, this became redundant with the introduction of franking credits. Now instead of a partnership you can have a company which pays tax and then pays a franked dividend to the shareholders. The shareholders then claim the franking credits against their personal tax.

Private company

A limited private company is limited in its responsibilities. Its shares may not be offered to the public, and the red tape is a lot less than that for a public company. The advantage is that it limits the liability of the shareholders to their investment in the company. It is easy to transfer ownership by selling shares and shareholders can be employed in the company. The downside is that it is often hard to find a buyer for the shares. The shares are illiquid.

Public company

A company whose shares are traded freely on the stock exchange. Its shares are liquid.

Not-for-profit organisation

A not-for-profit organisation is one that does not operate for profit, personal gain or other benefit of particular people. If eligible it may be able to receive tax deductible gifts.

Incorporated association

An incorporated association is a legal entity separate from its individual members and can hold property, sue and be sued. Incorporating in a state or territory restricts the organisation to operating in its home jurisdiction.

Discretionary trust

A discretionary trust is one in which the number of shares of each beneficiary are not fixed by the settlor in the trust deed, but at the discretion of the trustees.

Testamentary trust

A testamentary trust is one that arises upon the death of the testator, and which is specified in his or her will. A will may contain more than one testamentary trust, and may address all or any portion of the estate. To really understand testamentary trusts, you have to understand the law and human nature. What happens is that someone comes up with a great idea to help those in need and that legislation is taken to the limit and used as a tool for the formation and nurturing of intergenerational wealth.

So the original idea was that in the case mum and dad had a child with serious learning difficulties, the parents judge that the child will never be able to look after themselves so they set up a protective testamentary trust. That means that when the parents die the money will be held in the care of nominated trustee who will pay the money out as the child requires. This means that another person cannot come along and take advantage of the child and take all their money. Great. What happens if the parents die when the child is very young.

Superannuation fund

Superannuation is the portion of your earnings and savings that is placed in a fund to be held in trust until your retirement. The objective of superannuation is to provide income in retirement that substitutes or supplements the Australian Age Pension.

A self-managed superannuation fund is a way of saving for your retirement. The difference between a SMSF and other types of funds is that the members of the SMSF run it for their own benefit and are responsible for complying with the super and tax laws.

The Australian Super Guarantee System started in 1992. As a result, middle-aged middle Australians are now in a position where they have substantial savings in their superannuation accounts. Today, Australians have around $3 trillion in super funds.

Types of super funds

Industry funds
Corporate funds
Self-managed super funds (SMSFs)

Expected returns of super funds and LICs

The average investment return of Australia's super funds over the past 22 years (that is, from inception) has been 7.1%, while the average annual total return from the Australian share market over the same period has been 10.4%. That's not great, but it's OK, given the asset allocation imperatives of large-scale investing. The sole purpose of a super fund is to provide for its members' retirement.

At 7.1% compound growth per year over 40 years, a worker on the average wage paying 9.5% of salary into super would end up with about $1.2 million. At 10% compound (the average total return from the share market over the past 22 years), the worker on average earnings saving 9.5% of salary over 40 years would end up with $3m—enough to fund a long and comfortable retirement (plus a cruise or two). Surely 10% per year compound should be the industry's aim for its customers—not 7%; 15% ($14m over 40 years) would be even better, but 10% should be a minimum benchmark.

It's a matter of expertise. Anyone can hug the index, pay themselves a fee and then give the index return minus the fee. The only way to achieve global leadership in any industry is to be good at it. In the business of investing that means valuing companies, and other assets, accurately, buying them at the right price, and then owning them with discipline. In my view, the way to achieve global leadership in investing is to skew the fees towards paying for performance. Paying a simple base fee produces base performance: people will always do what their salary tells them to do. So the main question is, if the Index did 10.4% why is it that that funds averaged 7.1%? The answer is in how the finance industry works.

- You as an employee chose a fund. It could be an industry fund, a corporate fund or a retail fund, it could also be your SMSF.
- That fund manages your investments. It is the fund manager. In the case of an SMSF, the manager is normally a financial consultant, financial adviser or accountant with a financial manager's ticket.
- Fund managers charge between 0.5–1.5% to administer the fund.
- The next step is to prepare an investment strategy. Every fund needs an investment strategy. This is normally done by a financial institution. In the case of some of the large funds they do it for you.
- Fund managers charge for the investment strategy. When you are asked if you want a conservative, growth, or high-growth fund, you pay for the advice of the actual strategy. In the case of a large fund, that price is difficult to nail down. In an SMSF, it is easier and can be around 0.5% of assets.
- You then choose an investment manager. There are many of these and big funds share the love around in the name of diversification. Look at what CBUS is paying Colonial First State Asset Management to manage their cash deposits. The asset manager charges between 1–2% to manage your funds in that vehicle.
- These investment managers then invest the money in tradable stocks, property or cash products. Many of these products charge a management fee for investing the money. LICs' MER can vary from 0.1–2.5%.
- So now it is time to add it all up.

- The fund manager: 1%
- The strategy manager: 0.5%
  The investment manager: 1%
- The investment administration: 1%
- Custodian expenses: 0.5%
- **Total: 4.0%**

Hence an investment such as AFIC has an average return of 11.4% (inclusive of franking credits.) over the last 29 years and the average super funds have an average return of 7.4% to their clients. So while saying that the funds need to invest better to enhance their returns, they also need to reduce the fees taken in the process.

Let's put that simply. If you have $500,000 in your fund today, you add $15,000 a year for the next ten years. At 6.29%, that is the 7.4% after tax, your balance will be $1,144,432 or $891,517 after inflation. At the same time if your return was 11.4% less tax equals 9.69%, your balance will be $1,564,095, or $1,218,435 after inflation.

To make it easy, taking the raw figures you will earn another $419,663 over a 10-year period or $40,000 a year after tax. So the question to you is whether it is worthwhile spending some time and energy earning another $40,000 per year. However, as you get older it becomes even more complicated. The differential in costs is about 4%, which is $20,000 on a $500,000 portfolio. What happens if that portfolio was worth $2m? Then the differential is $80,000 after tax and of course on a $10m portfolio a difference of $400,000 after tax per year is significant.

The question then becomes, when is it more efficient to retire and manage your own affairs than continue at work? The answer to that is in the balance of finance, lifestyle, job satisfaction and kudos. You do have to consider that if you retire to manage your own affairs you are still open to get other jobs with more job satisfaction and a better lifestyle.

Legal Structures

You need to think long and hard before setting up any structure because it will have a significant effect on your positions in the future. There are issues of tax, intergenerational wealth and partnerships. When you look at the structure of large corporations, you will find a number of different entities that are interconnected. In the construction or development business you will see that each project has a different entity. If one project goes broke it does not bring the whole structure down.

What you do need to know is that each entity has a set of rules that used to be called the articles of association, now called the constitution or in the case of a trust the trust deed. Each have their pros and cons. What you must keep in mind is your long-term objective. The trust that my grandfather started for my mother in the 1940s seemed like a really good idea at the time but turned into a nightmare 50 years later.

The Concept of Wealth

There are many definitions for the concept of Wealth. In economics, net wealth refers to the value of assets owned minus the value of liabilities owed at a point in time. That is wealth is measured as a balance sheet item. I would prefer to think of wealth more in terms of the P&L. To me you are wealthy if you have enough income to cover your expenses. That is at the end of each month there is money in the bank. A wealthy person is one who makes a dollar each month more than they spend.

In our balance of life that can also have negative connotations. It can mean to stay wealthy that you have to work long hours for the rest of your life. Surely that is not being wealthy. Working hard to make enough to pay for your life and luxuries is great, but at some stage you are going to want to sit back and enjoy your "wealth". So, under those circumstances, what does wealth mean?

Unearned income

Unearned income is the income you receive as a result of your investments, not because of your daily labour. Unearned income is the dividend income from shares, the rent income from an investment property, the distributions from a trust or the interest from cash in the bank. This is the income you receive from the savings from your previous labour. It is the income you earn from the labour you put into investing those savings to get a maximum return.

The real definition of wealth to me is when your unearned income meets your cash requirements for your living expenses as you would like to live. This for a simple person could be a few hundred dollars a week, for a celebrity superstar it could be in the hundreds of thousands a week.

The point is that to feel good about yourself and your family you only need one dollar more than what it takes to run your life. This then becomes a crucial investment goal: to build up enough unearned income for your retirement so that you can live the life you dreamed of.

Lazy money

It is pointless being wealthy in terms of having a huge asset base, if that asset base is not providing you with an unearned income for you to enjoy. Similarly, it is pointless in your accumulation phase to be putting yourself and your family under financial pressure to save, if you do not make that money work for you.

Creating wealth

As soon as we mention creating wealth the vast majority of Australians turn off, I am not sure why. Probably some think that is not me, others are just plain scared. First of all, you need to really understand what wealth is. We have discussed this in detail.

Let's look at some figures based on the superannuation

guarantee charge (SGC) if you leave school at the age of 18 and do a four-year university degree and then go to work at age 22 on an average graduate salary.

Assumptions:
1. You put in $1,900 a year while at uni.
2. The starting salary is $50,000.
3. You have CPI increases until age 68.

During that time, you will have earned $4,463,394 and made contributions of $424,022 into your super fund.

Now, if your fund returns 6% for the whole career, your balance will be $1,794,336, but if your fund returns 8% the balance will be $3,258,611. Even allowing for CPI increases that is still around $1m in today's dollars. So the point is that wealth is not too far away. Of course, if you average a rate of return of 10%, your balance would be $6,161,417.

So, even the average graduate can become wealthy if they get a few things right.

What do we need to get right? There are four factors.

Generation of capital

Capital can be generated by saving, inheritance or even winning lotto. In most cases the capital is created through savings, which is a function of budgeting and frugal living.

Savings is not always a function of your income. There are many people on low incomes that manage to save reasonable amounts of money and plenty of people on very high incomes that cannot save a dollar.

Generation of Capital as a function of Income.

As we have seen above, wealth creation is not a function of income. In fact, a large income can have an inversely proportional effect on wealth creation. In the finance sector, barristers, airline pilots, dentists and doctors are all famous for being poor at wealth creation. There are a number of reasons for this.

1. Some people think that lifestyle purchases are assets. Robert Kiyosaki was famous for saying that your principal place of residence is a liability and not an asset. Well, not only do I agree with him but I will go one step further: all lifestyle purchases are liabilities. The definition of an asset in financial terms is a thing of value that produces an income stream. Your house, holiday house, car, boat do not produce income streams and are therefore not assets.

   Now, many of you are going to say I will build a big house and sell it later to get tax-free money to buy a smaller house and invest the rest. Think again. Once you have lived in a great suburb in a house with all the mod cons, even a smaller replacement is going to cost you the price of the house and on top of that any money left over will be required for body corporate fees.

   What the great believers in house wealth will not tell you is that to keep a house up it requires at least 2% of the value each year in maintenance to keep the house to standard. That 2% is in after-tax dollars, your mortgage payments are in after-tax dollars, the rates and expenses are in after-tax dollars. I am pleased to sit down with you and a spreadsheet at any time and show you just how much a valuable house is costing you. A bit like dueling laptops instead of dueling banjos.

2. People with high incomes tend to think the incomes will come forever. This is where the majority fall over. They have heavy borrowings and focus on their income tax issues without focusing on the balance sheet. We have said creating wealth is about a slow increase in equity. That means every year you need to be assured that your equity is increasing. Many fall into the trap

of borrowing more and increasing their liabilities. Then when the music stops they are left with little or nothing.

3. Strategies of high-income earners tend to revolve around heavy borrowings. This can lead to high risk on two levels. The first is that the assets will fall in value and you will be unable to fill the gap. The second is that the income will stop unexpectedly.
4. High-income earners tend to focus their structure around today and not the future. This often leads to substantial problems down the line. Greg Norman believes that visions should encompass a 100-year horizon. That is about four generations down the track. To have a structure to suit that sort of objective, you need to think it through very clearly.

Rate of return

You are aware of the power of compound interest. Let's put that into perspective right now. At age 28 you have been frugal, saved, and have $25,000 in your pocket. You have already made plans for your house deposit so you think let's go buy a car. You have two choices: buy a $5,000 car and invest $20,000 or buy the $25,000 car.

If you invest the $20,000 at 6% for 40 years you will have $220,000, but if you get a return of 10% you will have $1.1m. What a difference.

There is a direct relationship in investing between risk and return. The higher the risk, the higher the return. Remember it is not a risk of losing the money it is the risk of volatility.

We have shown that rate of return is not only a function of risk, it is also a function of the fees that are pulled out. The lazy person puts their money in a managed fund and lets somebody else look after it for them. But if you manage it yourself, you can get the higher return without actually having to take on more risk.

The rate of return is a function of the investment return minus the costs and tax.

Structure

Structure is a function of objectives, timeframe, taxation and succession planning. There is an old story about somebody going by Rolls Royce to a meeting with a Wall Street firm, wondering why they are taking advice from someone who got to work on the train. Before someone can advise you, they need to be able to climb into your shoes.

We have discussed how computers have ruined science, economics and law. A combination of computers and regulations has ruined good structural advice. Advisers these days are more focused on making sure the advice they give is according to the regulations set down by the regulatory bodies than they are of actually finding the best fit for you. No two people will have the same desires or objectives, yet financial planners, accountants and lawyers tend to give you a one size fits all product.

Your long-term plan is the key to structure, and your structure is a key to the success of your long-term plan. In 20 years' time, what will your earned income be, what will your unearned income be, and who will be dependent on you?

Strategy

Your strategy will include your generation of capital(savings), the highest possible rate of return and the right structure to achieve your goals.

Set your vision

By now, you will have gathered that you will never go anywhere if you do not have a vision. Your vision comes from all the work you are about to do in the next chapter. You need to define who you are and then create your ideal vision balanced against the five aspects of your life.

Plan to achieve your vision

Your success is measured by your performance against your plan. The plan will keep you in line and make sure you use self control during the tough times.

Pick your specialties.

You will always be better at something you really like doing. You have to believe in something if you want it to work. There are going to be many times in your plan when it is only your belief that is going to keep it together; without that belief you will give up. That means that you need to invest in things that you know are going to work. House prices have been going up for the last 3,000 years, so what is the chance they are not going up in your lifetime? The share market has been going up for the last 200 years; why would it not go up when it is linked to the future profits of the world's economy?

Scott Adams would tell you that 90% of decisions are emotional and you later use logic to validate your decisions. Most people buying a house would agree with that. You go in with great thoughts of checking the power and the plumbing. Which way it faces and all the rest. But you buy the house that you walk in to and say "this is home". You will find the same with your specialty. Are you emotionally attached to real estate or shares or bitcoin?

Pick your Specialists.

The investment world is far too complex for any retail investor to come to grips with. In order to invest well you need to measure the companies or properties and that takes time effort and influence. The average retail investor does not get to walk into the offices of most listed companies. It also requires technical knowledge in this age of digital trading. You can get caught very quickly.

Therefore you need to find a specialist to do it for you. We have seen that these come in many shapes and sizes, but your job is to find the operators that you believe in, that you have faith in and that have a track record. Your job is to find the specialist not make individual investments.

Most people do not get excited about going through a whole lot of figures in finance reports. So why don't you look at it from a human resources point of view and not an analytical one. The job is to outsource your requirements and therefore it is a social and psychological issue and not a mathematical one. It took me sometime to find the right key.

Intergenerational wealth

This is a subject that has strong roots in mythology, religion and governance structures.

There are still many faiths where the wealth of a family is passed to the eldest son of the next generation. Monarchies married families together so as to combine wealth. Families went to extreme lengths to ensure that the wealth of the family is kept together. There is a very good reason for this and that is that in order for a major project to be successful you need a critical mass of assets. History tells us that many of the great buildings were built over a number of generations. Nations and enterprises have been built over many generations. If half way through the process the family splits the assets up then the project comes to a grinding halt.

This all happens because of the instinctive nature of humans. In the twentieth century when the concept of equality was developed the movement of wealth through generations was first questioned and then stopped by inheritance taxes, capital gains tax, land tax and others. Therefore a bunch of assets owned by a family was stripped by the government. Wealthy families reacted in a post modern egalitarian way. Instead of passing down their wealth to the first born son they split it up to all the family. This is one of those really important points you need to digest. When the family capital was split it tended to be used for the purchase of lifestyle assets instead of as investment capital. The head of the family would normally break it up when they were getting into their 80's. At that stage they had three children who each had two children. That is nine direct descendants who are adults. More often than not the grandchildren are in their late 20's to 30's. By this time the family had learned to live well and wanted houses in the best parts of town. The family fortune is split up there are 9 new houses and nine new cars purchased. For the normal family that would mean the whole capital base has been eroded and used for non income producing assets. Hence the socialist system gets its way.

There are many ways to attack the issue of intergenerational wealth. The very rich sometimes give it away, such as Gates and Buffett. There is the adage that says leave the kids enough money so they feel they can do anything, but not so much as they can do nothing. Everyone will have their own version of what that may mean. They will also have their own definitions of exactly how they do want to help their children without in fact hindering them.

There have been many family court cases where children have demanded more inheritance, or parents have been too generous. It is noticeable that those in the entertainment industry tend to struggle, while those in hard industries tend to do a lot better. In many ways, this comes back to the basic values and beliefs of the parents. Those with liberal progressive values tend to ruin the lives of their children while those that have had it tough themselves tend to make the children work for their heritage.

Your thoughts on intergenerational wealth will be a part of your psychological profile. You need to be very clear on your own profile before you can start to put together a structure that will meet your objectives. At the same time, you may have inherited a structure that rules the way you act to a certain degree.

You must always keep in mind that the world is changing and therefore while wanting to "rule from the grave", you must also create enough degrees of freedom for your children to move around new legislation and regulation.

I would argue that if you have taken on responsibility for yourself at an early age you will then take on responsibility for your family during your lifetime. But that doesn't have to stop.

Intergenerational wealth structure

I have learned there are five major issues with achieving intergenerational goals.

1. There needs to be a family member with passion through the generations. Sometimes it skips a generation and that doesn't matter.
2. The funds need to be kept in a single structure. Once you break it up into a myriad of trusts and testamentary trusts, the capital disappears into individual dreams and aspirations and suddenly it is gone.
3. The lead entity, must have a constitution that requires, in order of importance:
    a) Capital growth in line with CPI.
    b) Capital growth of 3%, in excess of CPI, to allow for the growing family.
    c) Capital gains tax needs to be paid along the way. A massive CGT bill in the future will ruin any good structure.
    d) Income distribution to achieve individual goals: (1) The ability to take a distribution in cash; (2) The ability to reinvest in the unit trust.
4. The Operational Entity, a discretionary trust, must have the flexibility to distribute income to where it is required when it is required.
5. The discretionary trust needs a corporate beneficiary that can balance out distributions during good and poor years.

The vision: To use family capital to support the education, housing and retirement of future generations. (If you cannot look after yourself on a daily basis, that is your problem.)

Step 1. The Family Discretionary Trust. Aims:

1. To provide a family maternity leave payment. To provide for the education of future generations. To establish an adolescent allowance for 4 (four) years to:
    a) Teach budgeting skills.
    b) Provide financial relief to parents.
    c) Start a superannuation fund.
    d) Act as a conduit to independence.
2. Start a superannuation fund for the next generation.

Socialist v Capitalist

The socialist way is for the parents to go skiing and leave none of their capital to their children. Everyone should be equal and as our former treasurer now Prime Minister said of the superannuation scheme nobody should be allowed to use it for the transfer of intergenerational wealth.

Under that system all the family money is spent and future generations join everybody else where 85% of retirees are on a pension or part pension being paid for by 20% of the population. Now that's equality.

The capitalist would say. It is my responsibility to look after my family now and in the future. So the young capitalist will start their super fund on graduation day at the age of 22. If they get an average salary of $55,000 and pay into a retail or industry fund returning around 6% then at the age of 68 they will have $1.1million in their account. Allowing for a 2.5% inflation that would be about $380,000 or the average fund today. However if our young capitalist spent some time on their own SMSF and managed to return 8% then they would have $2.1mill or about $700,000 in today's dollar terms. Now lets say they did a bit more work and managed to return 10% they would have $4.1mill or

$1.4mill in today's terms.

Of course when they retired at 68 that gave them an income of $400,000 which they didn't need so they left $200,000 in the SMSF and continued on for 10 years. By the time they were 78 they had a balance of $15mill. Now this $15mill was left to the 9 grandchildren who shared the income which meant that not one of them was eligible for any government entitlements.

All of you need to make the choice. It is not difficult to devote enough time to investment structures and returns such you will be able to support your families for generations to come all you need to do is pick the load up and carry it. On the other hand you can swim with the masses and end up as a welfare beneficiary at the will of the government. Your choice.

Hero or zero

The following stories have been printed many times.

Grace Groner was born in 1909 in rural Illinois. Orphaned at age 12 and never married, she began her career during the Great Depression. She became a secretary, lived in a small cottage, bought used clothes and never owned a car. When Groner died in 2010, those close to her were shocked to learn she was worth at least $7 million. Even more amazing, she made it all on her own. The country secretary bought $180 worth of stocks in the 1930s, never sold, and let it compound into a fortune. She left it all to charity.

A Wall Street hero ... now zero

Now meet Richard Fuscone. He earned an MBA from the University of Chicago. Rising through the ranks of high finance, Fuscone became Executive Chairman of the Americas at Merrill Lynch. *Crain's* once included Fuscone in a "40 under 40" list of successful businesspeople. He retired in 2000 to "pursue personal, charitable interests." Former Merrill CEO David Komansky praised Fuscone's "business savvy, leadership skills, sound judgment and personal integrity." But Fuscone filed for bankruptcy in 2010 – the same year Groner's fortune was revealed – fighting to prevent foreclosure of his 18,471-square-foot, 11-bathroom, two-pool, two-elevator, seven-car-garage New York mansion. This was after selling another home in Palm Beach following a separate foreclosure. "My background is in the financial-services industry and I have been personally devastated by the financial crisis," Fuscone's bankruptcy filing allegedly stated. "I currently have no income." These stories fascinate me. There is no plausible scenario in which a 100-year-old country secretary could beat Tiger Woods at golf, or be better at brain surgery than a brain surgeon. But – fairly often – that same country secretary can out-finance a Wall Street titan. Money is strange like that.

The point is that you can become wealthy on the minimum wage and you can end up bankrupt with a huge wage and a huge amount of assets.

Creating real wealth is a long slow process. OK, I admit there are some that make it quickly: they get into the right business at the right time and suddenly they have a huge amount of assets.

The Future

Just when you think you are safe something comes and hits you from the side. In my lifetime, Australian manufacturing, along with many unskilled job opportunities have been greatly reduced. The call centres went overseas, and now more and more jobs are departing our shores.

Superimpose on that the fact that technology is making huge changes to the traditional distribution channels. We are starting to see business being closer and closer to the seller and buyer doing a direct transaction instead of going through a number of intermediaries.

I predicted the end of managed funds a number of years ago. Why would you pay all those businesses to take more in fees than they add to the chain? The Warren Buffett bet against the hedge funds put the final nail in the coffin for a class of active fund management. The risks are too high and the returns have not been great. Over the next decade, we will see the following happen in the investment world:

1. Financial advice will be computerised. You will go online, fill in a bunch of boxes and out will pop your new portfolio.
2. The funds you invest in will be ETFs with next to no fees. You will buy the market. That means you will take a stake in the growth corporations of the day.
3. Computerisation will bring arbitrage to a halt.
4. The derivatives industry will become one big computer game before the real investors realise that it is just computerised gambling.
5. Bank loans will be online, the same as financial advice.
6. Bank branches will disappear completely.

Those are just a few of the things that will definitely happen. Now for the things that could happen.

1. Money as we know it will disappear.
2. Shares in companies will disappear and therefore there will be no stock markets.
3. Large companies will be replaced by a mass of digitally connected single operators.
4. Governments will change from the single leader to an aggregated mass form of leadership.

I know that wading through all the political, economic and cultural material in Part I was tough going, but it is in this situation that we bear the fruits of digesting all that material.

You will know that we are living in a world changing at a rapid rate; you will know that the old businesses are being left in the wake of new start-ups; you will also know that buying and holding assets is a tough gig in today's world, and therefore Walmart may be a really bad investment. On the other hand, if a new disruptive business comes along in the next decade, Amazon being nothing but an income stream could be worth just that, nothing. This is why it is so important that you understand the environment in which you are living.

8
Who are you?

This is the part you have been waiting for. It's all about you. However, if you think you can skip all the boring stuff in the first two parts you are dead wrong. Read this material without understanding your environment and learning the basics of investment and business and you will learn little.

You as an individual

We have looked at the world, Australia, the family and now it is time to look at yourself. It is incredibly difficult to look at yourself for who you are and not who you want to be. You may go to a party and sit on the outer dreaming of being the extrovert at the centre of attention or you may be the sprinter that flies at new challenges but runs out of steam all the while hoping you were the marathon runner with endless persistence. Being true to yourself is one of the most difficult things you will do. At this point in your development you need to understand yourself to set reasonable goals. You can change your desires, but it is much harder to change your personality.

Personality

In really old times, about 20 years ago, the test used for determining personality was the Myer-Briggs test (MBTI). This test divided the personality into four dichotomies.
1. Your favourite world. Extroversion (E) or Introversion (I).
2. Information. Sensing (S) or Intuition (N).
3. Decisions. Thinking (T) of Feeling (F).
4. Structure Judging (J) or Perceiving (P).

After doing the test you have your own personality type which will be one of 16 possible types, eg, ENTP. The Myers-Briggs web site explains in full and you can do the test.

In modern times the Big 5 Personality Test is the most commonly used model of personality in academic psychology. The test takes 3 to 8 minutes to complete and is free online. The five factors identified are:

1. Openness to experience.
2. Conscientiousness.
3. Extraversion.
4. Agreeableness.
5. Neuroticism.

You need to try the tests and get a feel for your personality.

Values

Your personal values are the core of what you are, and who you want to be. By understanding your values, it is easy to make decisions in many situations. Sometimes you really have to ask yourself what you really value before being able to be content with a difficult decision. You will use your values to define what you think is right and wrong. Who you are is the most important thing in your life, the reason for that is that you need to be able to wake up every morning look yourself in the mirror and tell yourself you are on track and OK.

Some years ago, I had a cancer scare and had surgery to remove a "mass". In the days leading up to the operation, I had time to reflect on my life to that point. If this was the end was I happy with who I was. At another point in my life I woke up one morning, looked in the mirror and was not impressed with what I saw. I needed to change and to change: I needed a plan.

Your values need to be written down, we are all different. A list of possible core values can be found at http://jamesclear.com/core-values. The author suggests you pick the five that are most important to you. At this point your inner self will be struggling against your need for kudos. It is really important that you understand your own personal core values, as your plan is going to push you in their direction. If you try to fool yourself, your plan becomes impotent.

You need to choose several core values and then define a measurement for each of them. There is no point in defining a core value but not being able to measure how you have done in relation to it. There will be times when you may wish to change a core value; in fact, I would suggest that it is probable that in the first ten-year plan you will change a number of core values. When you are young, you tend to want to be popular. Being liked and admired by others is important to most adolescents. When you start to grow and have a family of your own, your focus will change and popularity may be replaced by self-respect. Who cares whether you are liked or not, if you can like yourself? Your values are the soul of the plan.

Beliefs

A belief is a state of mind in which a person thinks something to be the case, with or without there being empirical evidence to prove that something is the case with factual certainty. We are not going to get into a philosophical discussion about opinions, beliefs, knowledge and the continuum between them. All we need to know is that as we travel through life our beliefs will change as we gather more evidence. Some beliefs will be enhanced and others thrown to the wind. There is a saying alleged to have come from Winston Churchill, "If a man is not a socialist by the time he is 20, he has no heart. If he is not a conservative by the time he is 40, he has no brain." This is an example of beliefs changing as you gather evidence.

I would argue that with 30 years' experience, if your beliefs haven't changed you need to have a good look at yourself. Where do you stand?

So, if you have a set of values, do not set them in concrete. For every action, there is an equal and opposite reaction. When setting values, you have to remember the third law of motion. If you believe in the free market, you have to believe in people taking responsibility for themselves. If you believe in big government, you have to believe in high taxes and government control.

When looking at yourself you need to have a path to follow. It has been well documented that the more specific the goal the better the chance you have of achieving that goal. By nature, humans want to achieve. Therefore, if you measure something by nature you will want it to improve. I was taught that every vision needed to be quantified and have a time frame. Visions of being the best at something are "motherhood statements" that mean nothing. A vision of achieving a measurable outcome on a certain date is a finite aim, you either pass or fail. Having said that remember failure is good. Successful people fail at lot more than unsuccessful people, why? Because they do more and they set more targets. I want to be the best student I can be means nothing, you neither succeed nor fail. Whereas "I want to get my degree with distinction" is a finite goal. You may or may not achieve that goal but you will do better than if you had no quantifiable goal.

Politics

Are you left-wing or right-wing, remembering left-wing means you accept or support social equality, and right-wing means you believe that naturally there is social inequality. It is not a question of are we all equal, or should we all be equal. Anybody that has played in a school yard knows that we are not all equal. There are the natural leaders and there are those that are always picked last, that is a fact we cannot get away from. The question is, do you believe we need a system of government that leads us to social equality?

The key issue for the left wing is where to draw the line. If you believe that we need a system of government that has concern for those who are perceived to be disadvantaged relative to others, how do you define disadvantage? On the right wing, if you believe there is a natural social stratification or social inequality, how far do you let that run? If you accept that some people are less capable of providing for themselves than others where do you draw that line?

In relation to social philosophy, are you a conservative and believe that present values have been defined over centuries and should stay where they are. Or are you a progressive who believes that economic and technological development dictates a need to change social values. Some would argue the churches of the world had been too conservative in hanging onto outdated values. Others would argue that progressives have changed values without a reference to the tried and true and have therefore moved their position too far too quickly.

When is it time to change the rules? Two generations ago it was a general rule that age should be respected. It was generally believed that people who had lived a long time had grown in wisdom and knowledge and that those people had valuable input for the young to learn from, be it right or wrong. The seismic change in technology has changed that to a position where the young believe that they know more than the older generation. They believe the rules have changed so much that experience in the old rules and systems have no value. It is difficult to believe that centuries of learning have no value. So where do you put the stake in the ground.

A liberal believes in freedom of speech, free markets, civil rights, democratic societies and secular government. Socialists believe in social ownership and democratic control, while communists believe in state ownership of everything where there is only one class.

Financial

I read an article out of Harvard University, while studying for an MBA, which concluded that the top CEOs in the US only spent 20 hours a year on their own finances. While I applaud the fact that they totally focused on their well-paid jobs it seems relevant that they are focused on their company while paying scant attention to their own lives.

In that vein, I made up an Excel spreadsheet that took the super of the average graduate. By the age of 68 years the average graduate would have earned $4.5m in wages and $4.5m in super unearned income at 9.3% return on capital. That does not take into account the tax equation where the personal income after tax will be substantially less than the unearned income after tax. It also does not consider that the unearned income will continue at a rate of over $400,000 per year for the rest of your life.

If you are a high wage earner you would argue that at 68 you may have earned $17m, or a massive average of $340,000 a year for 50 years. In that case at 9% you will have only earned $11m in unearned income, however if you consider the unearned income rolling on to the age of 85 then at 9% you will have earned $48m in unearned income against the $17m in earned income.

So why is it that 99% of the population spend years studying or learning, and then 35–80 hours a week in their earned income pursuits and have trouble putting any time or effort into the unearned income that is going to be the biggest financial driver of their lives. Well, no doubt the answer is balance. They like what they do for a living and they do not like studying finance. That argument carries a lot of weight except when told by people that do not enjoy their occupations.

So where do you stand? Should you be able to own your own home? Then should you be able to own a company that produces products or services? That leads to whether it is OK for private companies to own the roads, the power lines and the medical benefits schemes. You need to think of efficiencies, productivity, control and pricing. Are you a communist that believes the government should control markets and therefore pricing, or a socialist that believes the government should own the means of production, or a capitalist that believes in the free market and that ownership is best in the hands of private individuals.

Cultural

Cultural differences have increased over the last century from a difference in knowledge, beliefs, art and habits to include differences in morals, laws and customs. We now have Australians that do not respect Australian law or even the Australian flag. Is it OK to have different laws for different people? The downside of letting citizens have their own law is shown in the Middle East and in Europe. These communities divided by religion, law or cultures have invariably lead to civil war of one type or another. Where do you draw the line on one segment of society having a different set of rules to another?

Opportunities

A quote we use a lot, attributed to a number of people, is "There are those that make it happen, those that watch it happen and those that wonder what the hell did happen".

After defining your personality, values and beliefs you have to figure out whether you want to make things happen, watch or wonder. Making things happen is not for everybody, sometimes it is a bit like getting on a rollercoaster, there is the apprehension as you rise to the top. Then comes the point when you realise you are in for the ride and you cannot back out.

Opportunities come by you every day; you need to make the call as to whether you take them or let them go. Some people just sit on the couch with their face in a device and pretend those opportunities are not there. One thing I have learned is that there are many more opportunities that come your way than you will be able to take hold of. The other thing I have learned is that the really good ones come along when you do not think you can handle them.

On a business level I have had two major opportunities in my life. The first was when I was in Brisbane working in a small family company. We were trying to get a new product range off the ground to use a specific raw material. After having made samples and working to sell this product I was hoping to get orders for about a couple of thousand units. I was sitting opposite the customer when he gave me a forecast for a couple of thousand units per week. This was an opportunity.

I thanked the customer for his faith in us and got on the plane home. On the plane I thought, we do not have the raw material, we do not have the machinery, we do not have the expertise on the factory floor. Once I got home I discussed the opportunity with my partner, the first order was due in a month. We bought a third or fourth hand machine out of Perth, had it shipped to Brisbane and installed it ready to go in three weeks. Just enough time to get the first order out the door. That order led to a business that grew the business tenfold and focused on raw material that was nearly being thrown out.

The next really big opportunity came nearly 20 years later. I was running around the world trying to get business and flew back to the factory. I asked the team if there were any good leads on the emails, and a negative answer came back at me. Anyway, I sat down at the computer and went through the trashed emails, there was one that caught my eye. I went to my partner and we looked at it again. We instructed the manager to write back to the sender saying we could supply their needs. Within 20 minutes the phone rang from Taiwan: "When can we have samples." The initial samples got despatched the next day. They were followed up by a sample order of about 100 units. I flew up to Taiwan the next week to discuss the opportunities. I forget how many millions of units we made over the next few years, but it was enough to grow the business 20-fold.

While both these opportunities may look the same they were in fact very different although they did have in common that we needed to be alert, courageous and prepared to work very hard.

Threats

There are many things in life that are likely to cause you damage or danger. There is illness, injury, relationships and not least of all yourself. I would suggest the vast majority of your threats will come from you. Having said that the best way to deal with threats is to have risk-management plans in place to deal with potential threats. Hopefully by now you have a pretty good idea of who you are and what your potential downfalls are. For some there is a threat of reaching too far, and for others the threat of not reaching far enough.

Physical

There are the physical threats of illness and injury. These can be managed through behaviour and insurance.

Relationship

The relationship threats are great. We have said that you are likely to live to about 90 years of age. If you get married and have children late, it gives you a long time to pick the right partner. On the other hand, wait too long and you are likely to be miserable, driving around teenage kids when you are in your mid-50s. The other issue is that if you marry at 25, you are picking someone you are going to live with for 65 years.

Life expectancy has changed from 35 years of age to 90 but the rules of marriage have stayed the same. Many people in this era suggest that marriage should be only for 20 years and not for life. Whatever your thoughts, the law is pretty much the same. If you live with someone for 12 months they own half of you. That is a threat.

The same applies to whom you let into your business life. Con-people and charlatans are a threat, and you need to watch out for them. Many would say you are the company you keep. Constantly make yourself aware of your social environment.

Strengths

It can be really difficult to identify your own strengths. One management tool is to get people to do what they are good at.

What are your strengths?

Weaknesses

Most of us think we know our weaknesses, but in many cases, we do not. It is handy to listen to those that really know you well. The truth might be hard to stomach, but you owe it to yourself to actually hear it.

Strategic competitive advantages

This is the most important part of the process, actually determining what it is that you are good at. If you are going to be ahead of the pack then you need to work on your strengths and turn them into strategic competitive advantages.

Personally, I have an attention issue. If I had been born 40 years later I probably would have been diagnosed as ADHD. It was useless for me to get into a career that needed long hours at a desk with my head in books or on a screen. Writing this manual is probably the hardest thing I have ever done, hours upon hours on a single theme. It has been pure murder. That is why I originally studied geology: I knew I needed to be out in the field not stuck behind a desk somewhere.

A strategic competitive advantage for me is that I can deal with failure, not well, mind you, but I can deal with it. After all I have been supporting the Melbourne Football Club for the last 55 years. Being able to bounce back from failure is not just persistence, you must also have a degree of self-belief and a lot of passion.

At an early age, it is hard to know just what your advantages are because you have been raised in a group environment. I hesitate to say it but your age group has been brought up in the "everybody wins a prize" age, and therefore you will find it hard to actually know when you have a win as opposed to when one is handed to you. Natural ability is a must but then you have to work on that natural ability. We spoke elsewhere of footballers never reaching their true potential because they got paid too much too soon. The same applies to your strengths. You cannot take strengths for granted; you need to take them and work on them until they start to raise well above the average standard. Naturally talented people tend to fail later in life. That is because at school, it all comes so easily; they didn't have to work hard.

Conclusion

So, who are you? By now you must have a pretty good idea of who you are and where you are going.

I have to say at this time, that if you are a left-wing socialist progressive, there is really no point in going any further, because this process is all about making sure you are not equal with the majority, who have huge personal debts, spend their retirement on the pension, and roll about in the sea of life with no direction and no stability.

9

Your vision

In business, we have a *mission statement* that describes the business we are in and a *vision statement* that tells us where we are going. The vision statement must have a quantity and a date. A vision is useless if it is not quantified.

Now that you have found out who you are you need to find out where it is you are going.

Once you have defined your overall vision, you will need a vision for all five areas: job satisfaction, finance, lifestyle, kudos and morals/ethics. It is no good focusing on one to the detriment of the others; you will get out of balance.

I realise how hard this is so instead of sitting there staring at a blank sheet of paper I want you to write down on a sheet of paper a day in your life in ten years' time. This is not a vision, it is not a goal you will make a plan for, this is a dream of what you would like to become. After you have written the day in your life, you can pull out the different parts that are relevant to each issue and create a framework for your vision.

Are you a nomad or do you own a house? Are you in a relationship or living alone? Is work a major part of your life, or do you work to live? Do you have a whole heap of friends or just a few? Do you sleep well at night or have you made some decision you regret? This is about telling yourself who you want to be.

At this point you are going to ask, who does this? And the answer is the vast majority of the 20% of the population that will be self-funded retirees when you retire.

Remember you have a massive force against you. You have a

socialist government that wants to control your income and your capital. You have an elite force that wants to tell you what to think. You have a mainstream media that is throwing post-truth at you on a daily basis. You have a technical environment that is moving ahead much faster than you can keep up. If you do not have a strong belief in who you are and what you are doing, you will be swept up by the tide and become one of the majority being driven by external forces.

How do you win? You must have a strong game plan and the persistence to follow that plan. The plan will fall apart if you do not believe in it, and your belief will die if the vision is not based on your true values.

Total vision

The day in your life that you have described will lead to your total vision and your vision for each of the five elements.

The vision has to have numbers, and it has to have a time frame. Your total vision has to include visions for the following areas.

Job satisfaction

You will probably have three or four careers in your life. A great friend of mine once said. "It is daunting the first time you do it, it is exhilarating the next time you do it, it is exciting the first time you teach someone else to do it, and it is boring the 25th time you do it." No matter how you love what you do today, as time goes on that enthusiasm will wane and you will lose your love of the job. At that time, you need to move on. Many people do not realise this is happening until it is too late. That is why you need to get a measure of your job satisfaction, and be able to monitor that measurement.

Would you rather go to work and do the job, or do something else? When you start getting back late from lunch it is time to reconsider your level of job satisfaction

Lifestyle

As with job satisfaction, you will go through phases in your life. You cannot afford to get locked into a particular lifestyle. When I was a kid I loved the beach, now I find the sand intrusive. When young, you like loud music and wild parties, and as you mature, your likes will change. You need to establish a vision for your lifestyle with a KPI. If you can't measure it, it is not worth doing. I think that was Deming.

Finance

It is obviously much easier to measure a financial goal, but it is probably harder to set the goal in the first place. It is common for people to say that their financial goals tend to expand out as they get older. They will change as will your other goals.

Kudos

The need for kudos will also change as you move through life. When you are at school you want to be one of the cool kids; later on, you stop caring what other people think of you. I believe that is more a function of how you feel about yourself, than a function of how others feel about you. How many friends do you want? Some people want a handful others need many. What do you need?

Morals/ethics

Do you want to be a straight shooter or are you prepared to bend the rules? Is there a difference in morals and ethics for you. That is do you treat strangers the same as you treat your family or are you prepared to have a different set of values for family and friends.

10

Your plan

I need to point out this plan is for those that want to be self reliant. It is only for those that want to stand up and take responsibility for themselves and their family. So when it gets tough and it will, you have to look at yourself in the mirror and ask yourself who you are. Do not say you cannot do it, ask yourself how you are going to do it, and get the balance right.

Up to this point you have learned about your environment in a geographical, physical, political, financial and cultural sense.

The importance of planning cannot be over emphasised. A plan sets achievable goals and then shows you how to achieve those goals. Without a plan, we become like a rudderless ship just steaming along with no idea where we are heading. Many have found it not just important but necessary to put in place 10-year plans in their lives. Most highly successful people have a 10-year plan.

As Stephen Covey pointed out in *The 7 Habits*, you should "Be Proactive". That is, write the plan and then begin with the end in mind. Follow the plan. A friend of mine at age 75 is just putting his next 10-year plan in place. He is finding that instead of getting easier they are getting harder. As more people come into your life, spouses and children especially, the planning phase becomes more difficult and more complex.

Many will argue that you shouldn't need to plan, planning gives a rigid framework that stifles innovative and creative thinking. In my mind that is just a cop out. Your life plan is about you, you define the plan, you work out the essential elements of the plan and you put in place the actions that need to be done so that the plan is achieved.

Career

A career is defined as "an occupation undertaken for a significant period of a person's life and with opportunities for progress." You may have many careers in your life; for this plan you should be interested in the career you hope to have during the length of the present plan. The elements of a career are:

1. Occupation or job. This is something you are going to be doing for around 40 hours per week. As there are 168 hours in a week this is roughly 25% of your life. It is important you like it.
2. Significant period of time. A career used to last a lifetime but now it can last for as little as a few years. Normally a career would last for 20 to 30 years.
3. Opportunities for progress. Obviously different people will have different expectations in relation to progress. When I was about 17, my father sent me along to the personnel officer at BASF in Melbourne. Today that would be the Director of Human Resources. This guy explained to me that BASF had 350,000 employees worldwide. At the bottom level there were about 200,000, the next level 70,000, up a level more to 40,000 and so on. He then said, as long as you worked hard and kept on the road straight up, anyone could be the CEO when they reach 120 years of age.

What he said next has remained with me for the rest of my life, but it took me many years to grasp. He said, "Once you get to level three, there are more spaces above you than people that want to reach for them." This was a concept I found hard to embrace. However,

I saw it in everyday life. Most people do not want to go the extra mile. Many want to come to work and just do a job and then go home. In fact, for many, a job is a relaxing time away from the hurly burly of home where they can just relax do something and get paid.

If you sleep an average of eight hours a night then your work life is a third of the rest of your life, so you had better enjoy it. When it comes to choosing a career, many people start with what you are good at academically. I would argue that it is more important to understand what sort of lifestyle the career offers as opposed to the scholastic requirements. There are any number of parameters that you need to consider.

4. Working hours. Some jobs you can work 38 hours a week 9 to 5. Others will be 7 to 3, others will be shift work. Many jobs will require you to work at nights. The published hours are often very different to the reality.
5. Travel. Some jobs you go to the same place every day. Others you move from place to place. Others you are constantly on the move. The thought of travel can be very romantic, however when you have a number of small children, travel can be a relationship breaker.
6. Degree of socialisation. Will you be dealing with customers? Will you be working in a group or by yourself?
7. Degree of confrontation. In some professions confrontation is the norm. This is not restricted to the legal profession. Some people become customer service consultants and love dealing with angry clients all day every day. This is the same as those that choose a career in some forms of medicine, where you are dealing with death and dying all day every day, or police that spend their lives talking to social psychopaths that have no moral values and no empathy.

8. Working environment. There are exceptions to every rule and perhaps Steve Elkington was one of the best. Steve was a professional golfer who is allergic to grass, another would be my childhood hero, Admiral Horatio Nelson, who spent his life at sea but got sea sick in the tender going out to his ship. These are exceptions, the rule is make sure you are suited to your working environment. Those with claustrophobia do not do well in submarines. Those with ADHD do not do well in open plan working environments.
9. Size of employer entity. Some people work well in the structured and political environment of a big company, others find they work better in a more autonomous role.

Lifestyle

As we discussed earlier, in the early 1900s over 85% of the population was living in poverty and therefore a major criteria for any plan was to feed yourself and your family. The industrial revolution and the massive increase in productivity after the second world war meant that the focus of life changed from survival to other personal goals.

The 1960s, in the capitalist world, brought a whole new dimension to people's lives. San Francisco was the hub of the hippy revolution where for the first time in human history a whole generation looked at putting peace and love ahead of food on the table. Since that time, the hours in people's lives that were required for basic survival were diminished and lifestyle became more important than career.

It is hard for the adolescents of this era to understand the size of the change in how people live. I would guess that in 1960 the average Australian family ate out a couple of times a year. Many would use their holidays to paint their house or do the renovations or landscaping they had been planning. Most people had never been overseas and were never likely to go. The weekend meant mowing the lawn and going to the footy.

In lifestyle, there are the basic choices between those that want to live in the big cities, those for the smaller cities and those in regional areas. This is driven by any number of factors including their need for cafe lattes, and the theatre versus clean air and long drives with no traffic lights. We should never forget how lucky we are. There are still many in the world that do not have the opportunity of choosing where they live.

How you want to live your life needs to be defined and written down in the plan.

Finance

Your financial plan is only one of the five major issues in your plan, however without a solid financial basis at least three of the others will be hard to achieve. There are three stages to your financial life.

1. Your dependence on unearned income from your parents.
2. Dependence on earned income from your own labours.
3. Unearned income from your investments.

Where you are in this plan is dependent of which stage or stages you are in during the lifespan of this plan. For most, you will still be living off unearned income from your parents or family at the start of your first plan and then it will lead on to depending on the income from your own labours.

The Value of Money

It is easy to value money from the point of what it will buy, it is more difficult to value it from what it costs to collect. Money comes from work or trading. As trading takes work, I will focus on the money earned from work.

The 18-year-old at Macca's earns about $18 per hour, so you could say that a dollar is 3.33 minutes. However, the successful executive earning $400,000 per year values money at what? Someone on a salary such as that probably works 80 hours per week, say 48 weeks of the year. That would be $104 per hour, but at their marginal tax rate that would be $50 per hour.

The average university graduate has a starting salary of around $55K per year. They have four weeks' leave plus 14 public holidays. To be reasonably certain of an upwardly mobile career, they would work for nine hours a day. That's 226 days per year at nine hours per day or $27 per hour. At their marginal tax rate, that's $18 per hour. So, every extra hour for a Macca's worker is $18; for a graduate, $18; and for the high-flying exec $50. So let's look at what can be bought: say, a car.

The 18-year-old buys a second-hand Corolla for $1,000, or 56 hours. The graduate wants a new Corolla for $20,000, and that is 1,111 hours, or 28 weeks. The exec wants a $120,000 Merc. That will take 2,500 hours, or 34 weeks.

Cars, audio visual entertainment and holidays can be saved up for in a year or less: they are no big deal. But there are three expenses in your life that will require long-term planning, and they are:

1. A house.
2. Educating your children.
3. Your retirement.

The entry level for a house is about $350,000 out in the real world. On planet Sydney and Melbourne, well that is a different story. So a $70,000 deposit is required, and then $280,000 needs to be paid off in the next 20 years. A total of $350,000 in 30 years. To get the deposit, you would need to invest $380 per month for ten years at 8%.

Educating children

Depending on what type of schools, in what state and in what area the cost of educating a child runs from $5,000 per year up to $40,000. The main issue with educating children is the cash flow issue. Not only are you educating your children, but you are also trying to pay off your house and grow your capital base for your retirement. So having to find another $10,000 to $100,000 per year is not good timing.

Insurance

We all have dreams and then make plans to achieve those dreams. The plan never seems to go to plan; Murphy gets involved and things go wrong. Many years ago, when things went wrong the neighbours would gather around and help the unfortunate. Then we got bigger and that was not possible. Gambling has become a major part of our lives. There are those that are lucky and those that are not. More to the point there are those that know how to play the odds and those that do not. Our betting starts with a one on one bet, my footy team against yours. It then progresses to giving the other team a start, and later moves to playing the odds. In the betting game, there are the bookmakers, who make bets with the individual punters. The job of the bookmaker is to hedge the bets one against the other. The bookie hopes the outsider gets up so that they keep the funds from all the short-priced bets. In the game of life, we have insurance companies who take the individual bets. The job of the insurance company is to establish the risk of each bet and then price it accordingly.

During your journey to financial independence you move from a position where your assets and income are minimal and your dreams are big, to a point where your assets start growing and your income becomes the engine room. Your dreams have turned into objectives and you are gaining momentum. It is at this stage that you are most vulnerable. You have minimal assets, big dreams and a growing income. At this point you are dependent on that income and need to secure it. As time goes on your assets build and they need to be secured. You then move to having others that depend on you. During all this time, you have risks all around you. Political, financial, economic, natural events and destruction generated by other humans whether accidental or not.

These risks can be divided into four categories.

1. Those risks that are relatively unimportant, minor loss infrequently, can be retained. That is, you say, if that happens, well so be it, let's move on.
2. Those that are relatively important, A severe loss infrequently, can be transferred to someone else through insurance.
3. If they are bearable, those that are minor but happen frequently, you can work to reduce the frequency and self-insure, in other words bear the loss and move on.
4. For those that are severe and frequent, they are unbearable. That is, you cannot take the hit financially. These need to be eliminated or avoided.

The insurance industry divides these risks into general and personal risks. General insurance provides financial protection against loss or damage of stuff. Personal insurance covers you for life, death, trauma and sickness.

Divorce

As far as your financial plan goes, just do not have one. Divorce is by far the most crippling result for your financial plan. It is possible to have one really early in life and then pick up the pieces and move on, but later on, for most except the ultra-wealthy, divorce is the death knell for your financial life.

There are a couple of things you can do to avoid the pain of divorce and a pre-nuptial agreement is not one of them.

Choose your spouse very carefully. Make sure you share the same values and morals. Preferably share the same beliefs. Ensure a potential spouse is aware and in agreement with your long-term plan.

The other thing you can do is make sure that those who know you well meet your intended and you need to discuss the relationship with them in detail.

Family

Family is a complicated beast. There are many parts to it, and as you get older it becomes more complex. From my observations, the family unit is breaking down and I believe there is a simple reason for that. In the past, the young respected the older generations and wanted to learn from them. Today youth believes it has the answers and the elderly do not play a part in the future of the younger generations.

Superimposed on that are the geographical challenges of life when your career, your new family and your lifestyle takes you to different parts of the world. You are balancing a career and leisure activities, and there is no time or resources to uphold past traditions. All social groups need a driver, and the same is true with families. Without a driver, family gatherings become less frequent, until they tend to disappear altogether. The breakdown of the family gathering is a "first world problem".

Affluence has allowed smaller family units to travel and enjoy recreational activities in various parts of the world. When the geographical challenges are combined with people becoming more time-poor then the length and frequency of family meetings shortens. The family Christmas becomes a few hours instead of days. Family members fly in for the night to celebrate a birthday or an anniversary.

The result is that communication within the family becomes superficial, the shared interests become less and therefore there is less to communicate. The cycle begins until connection is lost and the family melds into the amorphous structure of Facebook, Twitter or Instagram, where there is no ongoing communication and no meaningful connection. In many ways, the friends on

Facebook become the ever-changing body of best friends taking the place of family.

So, what does your family mean to you? Can you define your relationship with your parents, your siblings, your grandparents and cousins? Do you have a need for family? Families cause pain; there is no doubt about that. Lack of family also causes pain. Which is the worst? Do you feel a responsibility to family? Do you even want a family? The point is that families are hard work, like all relationships. If you don't work on them, they die.

11

A Standard Plan

The Budget

It is not that difficult to budget properly and indeed to keep accurate records in the digital world that we live in. This is where the concepts of measurement and goals are so important.

Profit and Loss. With Previous Year Comparison.

			2019	2018
Income				
		Salary		
		Interest		
		Investment Return		
		Gifts		
Expenses				
Accommodation				
		Rent		
		Mortgage		
		Cleaning		
		Insurance		
		Pest Control		
		Rates and Taxes		
		Repairs and Maintenance		
		Electricity		
		Garden		
		Pool		

Total Accommodation			
Bank Charges			
Clothing			
Donations			
Entertainment			
Food			
Gifts			
Hobbies			
	Bike		
	Fishing		
Total Hobbies			
Insurance			
Legal Costs			
Medical			
	Medical Benefits		
	Refunds		
	Pharmacy		
	Dental		
	Doctor		
	Glasses		
	Other		
Total Medical			
Motor Vehicle.			
	Rego		
	R&M		
	Fuel		
Total Motor Vehicle			
Postage and Freight			
Subscriptions			
Telephone and Data			
Travel			

Wine			
Total Expense			
Net Income.			

The House

The Deposit

Given that you need a 20% deposit, that is $70,000 for a $350,000 house.

Start when you turn 18 and save $100 per week for 10 years invested at 7.2% and you get there.

If you can return 10% then you have enough for a $400,000 house.

Now if your family is into intergenerational wealth and your grandparents did some saving and gave you $20,000 at 18 to help along then you would have enough for a $600,000 house.

I realise that is not enough to buy a garage in the top spots in Melbourne and Sydney however the point is that if you budget, save and lead a frugal life you get to play the game. I cannot accept that it can't be done.

Start at 18 save $100 per week until you are 35 and invest it at 8% and you have $170,000, enough for a $850,000 house deposit.

I met a young man of 30 on a plane recently who was a maths teacher in a remote public school. I knew this was an outstanding person when I saw him doing quadratic equations on a note pad, that is with pencil and paper. He was married with 2 children owned his own house and had an investment property. The trick? He turned his passion for scuba diving into a business of under water welding performed during his holidays. Balance. Lifestyle, finance and job satisfaction. You can get it all if you plan it.

The Mortgage

At 30 you have the deposit and can buy that $350,000 house. Of course if you have partnered up you can have the $700,000 house, but let's keep it simple.

You buy the house $350,000 pay the costs and you are left with a $290,000 mortgage. Today that mortgage over 25 years will cost about $1,500 per month. At 30 you should be earning $65,000 per annum which is $56,000 per annum after income tax or $4,666 per month.

Your mortgage is one third of your income. You can do that.

In fact most people do not find this a problem. What they do find a problem is living in the house without doing the renovations, dining out 4 nights a week and going on two overseas holidays. Balance.

If you want a bigger and better house either earn more money or renovate yourself. Do not whinge that you can't afford to live in the area you would like to.

The Kids Education

Let's be really honest, this is when it really gets hard. This is not one of those feel good self help books that tells you that PMA will get you there. This step is the most difficult.

By itself it is not so hard but put in the context of starting educating the kids before you have paid off the house, well that leads to a whole lot of pain.

By this time you are 35 to 40 and the mortgage has reduced to 25% of your take home. The cost of educating the kids is the equivalent of another mortgage. So now you still have 5 years on the mortgage and have to double the outlay. Guess what many do. They borrow down on the mortgage and set themselves up for another 20 years of pain. Mid-life crisis here we come.

So what is the answer? Simple really start early, live in a house you can afford and get the mortgage out of the way before the major schooling costs kick in.

Who is yelling the loudest at the moment. That would be those that partied hard until they were 35, bought the big house they deserve at 38 and then settle into a 30 year mortgage and have children at the same time. The horse has bolted, gone, over the hill.

Those that have been paying attention will be saying. I saved from 18 to 30 for the deposit and then bought the house with a 25years mortgage. I am in pain from 35 to 55, and you would be right.

Now imagine that you graduated at 22 years old, get an average job at $50,000 per annum and start saving $1,500 per month. The same as you will have to with the mortgage. You already have about $22,000 from the $100 per week you have been saving and for the next 8 years you put in $1,500 per month. That means when you go to buy the house you will have $250,000 to put against the house. Buy a $400,000 house and the mortgage time is 10 years instead of 25.

That requires you to lead a frugal life, which can be as much fun as spending up big.

Superannuation and retirement planning

One of the taboo subjects today. Most people wake up when they are 50 and by that time the true value of compound interest has dissolved.

What is retirement? I don't think anybody really knows anymore. Most people are changing industries, or careers or occupations; they are not retiring. I like to think of it in an entirely different way.

What used to be called retirement is really the progression from earned income to unearned income. Earned income is the income you get from the tasks that you do daily, monthly or yearly.

Earned income comes in the form of salaries, wages, dividend income from a business in which you work or profits from things that you do. Unearned income is income from investments. It is income you receive whether you turn up for work or not.

During your life, there are three phases.
- Your dependence on unearned income from your parents.
- Dependence on earned income from your own labours.
- Unearned income from your investments.

The point is that from the day you start phase two you need to start thinking about phase three. The first question that needs to be asked is how much income you will need to match your desires. Then you need to figure out how much capital you will need to produce that amount of income.

Life Expectancy

There are many tables from which you can source this data. In rough figures those of you under 40 can expect to live to 83 as a male or 86 as a female.

Retiring Age

Charles Handy said in *The Empty Raincoat* that you will be educated until you are 25, work in direct employment until you are 45 then burn out and become a consultant until the age of 60–65 and then take on a mentoring role until the age of 75. You will then have ten years in "retirement" in which to reflect.

That means, for the lucky ones, you will be kept by your parents until you are 25. You will then need a high-paying job for 20 years to buy a home, educate kids and build a retirement fund. When you are 45 you will get a job as a consultant and earn enough to protect your lifestyle and continue to save for the future. At about 60, you will drop your income and start to rely on your unearned income. The key to this progression is that during the years from 60 to 75, you need to be building your unearned income and not diminishing the capital base from which it comes.

The need for retirement funding

1. How long?

In the 1960s, a 70-year-old was considered to have had a "good innings". In 2030, you will need to plan to living to 90+. This means you are likely to need to fund 30 years in retirement.

2. How much?

One of the greatest myths around is that you will live on 75% of your final salary in retirement. It simply does not work like that. When you are working, you get up and go to work, come home exhausted and nap in front of the TV. In retirement you spend time fixing things around the house and attacking new projects. These activities burn cash and provide no income.

3. Health

Health issues can result in health costs; they can also result in having to change your physical surroundings to be able to live.

4. Lifestyle

- Home. Are you going to live in the home you have built, or are you going to downsize, upsize, seachange or treechange?
- Hobbies. Retirement gives you the chance to spend time on those hobbies you would love to pursue. Guess what? They all cost.
- Relationships. Often relationships change in retirement. Some people slow down, some speed up, interests change and often your geographical location

changes. Finance is an important part of the equation. People want to do things but can they fund it? Planning trips and adventures is good, but will you all travel in the same class?

- Children. There has been a drift back to three generations living together. The grandparents look after the children while the parents go to work. This can be great or it can become a horrendous burden that makes retirement a drag. Many parents impress their values on their children and as a result commit to the expense of educating grandchildren or paying off mortgages or generally interfering in their children's lives.
- Most parents find it hard to see their children struggle financially. They have this desperate desire to help the kids. A general rule is that if your children are in trouble, they got themselves there. If you bail them out by paying off a mortgage, buying a new car or even funding holidays, they will buy a bigger house and a flasher car, and want better holidays. You exacerbate the problem.
- Legal structure. There are many issues that are involved in the funding of your retirement. Your tax structure. Your will. Power of attorney. Enduring power of attorney. Advance health directive.

Any analysis of your needs in retirement must end up with a retirement budget, a plan of how to finance the required income stream and a legal framework to ensure the plan stays in place as you age.

What are the options for retirement funding?

Basically, you need to make the choice as to whether you want to become a self-funded retiree or use the fallback position of the government pension. There is nothing in between.

The Status Quo

At present 80% of people over 65 years of age are on the pension or part pension. There are two tests for eligibility for the pension.

The **income test.** For a couple the aged pension will provide a base income of $653.50 per each or $1,307 per couple per fortnight or $33,982 per couple per year. For every dollar you earn over $288 per fortnight, the pension is reduced by 50 cents. That means that you will get a part pension up to an income of $2,902 per fortnight or $75,452. For example, if you as a couple earn $60,000 per year then you will get a part pension of $3,874 per year.

The **asset test.** This varies for homeowners and non-homeowners. For a homeowner, the pension threshold is $354,500. For every $1,000 in assets above that the pension is reduced by 75 cents a fortnight to an upper limit of $1,320,000.

There has been great discussion in the press about the millionaires that are paid a part pension. Well a couple with $1.1m in assets will get paid a pension of $94 a fortnight or $2,444 per year. Now for the rub. The test that gives you the lowest pension will apply.

Therefore, you could have $1m in assets well-invested earning 7% and you are out of the pension on the income test. Or you could have $1.5m in assets tied up in a family business earning very little and you will be ruled out on the asset test. The bottom line is that if you have assets over $1.3m or an income over $75,000 you can forget getting a part pension.

The point is that if you can live on $60,000 as a couple you are in play for living on a pension or part pension. If you have developed a lifestyle that requires more than that then you will have to join the 20% of those 65 and over that are self-funded retirees.

If you want to travel, have hobbies and lead the lifestyle you have become accustomed to then you have better plan on having an income more like $200,000 per year. With a 6% return on a super fund that will require a capital base of $3,333,333. If you can get 8% return, then the capital base would have to be $2.5m. Now the good news is that if you start when you are 20 years of age and put in the required superannuation guarantee (SG) amount on the average wage for 45 years you will meet your objective.

However, the bad news is that if you leave your SG in an underperforming fund then you will not reach your target. Obviously, you need to take inflation into account, but that is all part of the management and monitoring process. Over the years from 25 to 65 the balance will change from earned income to unearned income until the unearned income takes over as the primary source of income. You need to constantly monitor the situation.

The Point: Funding your retirement is the biggest, longest and most complex financial objective you will achieve during your life. You need to start the program from the first day you enter the workforce if not before.

How to achieve the objective?

The first part of any good plan is to outline the objective. It needs to be quantified and to have a timeframe. You need to fill in the gap. "I am committed to having an asset base of $X, with the ability to return an income of $Y per year by the time I am Z years of age."

Seriously this is the easiest objective of all the reach.

At a salary of $50,000 per year putting 9.5% into super with a net return of 6% over 40 years will give you an end balance of $800,000. Now the problem is you have to pay tax so the industry super fund 6% return becomes 5.1% an the end balance $630,000.

However if you get yourself some financial skills and return 11.5% with a net of 9.8% then you end up with a balance of $2.4million and you are set for retirement.

So the super fund gives you $630,000 invested at 7% an income of $44,000. Or you can do it yourself have a balance of $2.4million with a return of 8.5% giving an income of $204,000 per annum.

So the only question remaining is do you want to retire on $44,000 or $204,000. More importantly are you prepared to put the time and effort into getting the greater return.

Intergenerational Wealth Creation

Scenario 1

You were late off the mark with the deposit for the house. Then you succumbed to the renovations and poured all your savings into your principle place of residence. That means you are probably going to retire with the 80% and therefore when you sell the house and downsize you will either blow the difference or help the kids with their houses. Either way you do not have to worry about intergenerational wealth.

Scenario 2

You do all the right things. You pay the house off. Invest your super well and are in a position to help the kids without resorting to dipping into your capital. Great work. Now it comes to the end of your life. You leave the $2.4mill in super to the kids who immediately use it to upgrade their houses, buy new cars and help your grandkids with their houses. Your life's work will go up in smoke in 3 to 5 years. (I actually ran that past about 5 professional accountants working in the area. They all laughed and said 1 to 2 years more likely.)

Scenario 3

By the time you have the $2.4mill you have become old, cynical, arrogant, dictatorial and condescending. You will have developed a love and passion for your grandchildren as well as your children and possibly your great grandchildren. You will start to think like the monarchs of old. The assets cannot be broken up, yet you won't want to give them all to the eldest. You will want your legacy to grow not be thrown away and you will want freedom for your family and not have them locked into a structure that goes against their will or values. At the same time you are living in a socialist society that sees your wealth creation as wrong and a source of income for those that threw it all away.

Your objectives are:
1. Keep the assets together.
2. Grow the assets beyond CPI.
3. Allow those that want to opt out to do just that.
4. Ensure those wanting to opt out do not bring the structure down like the house of cards.

At this point I should put in 10 pages of disclaimers telling you this is not financial advice, you need to seek your own advice and this proposition may not be suitable for your circumstances.

The Structure

If you build your structure so that there is a unit trust at the head then you can gift units in that trust to each of your children in your will. You can write the trust deed such that the prime aim of the trust is to build capital at CPI plus x%. After that income is distributed to the unit holders.

Given your kids are smart then they will have their units in their own discretionary trusts and will be able to build their own wealth or spend it as required.

If one of the kids is either a complete spendthrift or so left wing they hate the presence of the trust they can get out by selling their units, or giving them to charity.

If they cannot find family members to buy the units then units could be sold outside the family, you don't care because your legacy will continue to grow.

Let's take your $2.4mill and grow it at CPI plus 2% for the 80 year life of the trust. That would be $12million is todays terms.

Scenario 4

If you are 65 and have been lucky to live in a world dominated by income and have earned a good salary of $150,000 for the last 30 years, and:

Started your own super fund 30 years ago at age 35 with $200,000.

Invested in a moderate risk environment to return 11.5%.

You will have $6.2mill in your super fund to retire on.

Add to that the fact that you resisted your family's desire to take them to Disney World 20 years ago. You put the $120,000 it was going to cost into a discretionary trust and invested it at a higher risk and returned 13% or 10% after tax. That gives you a balance today of over $700,000 with capital gains of over $400,000.

As your grandchildren turn 18 you can distribute to them capital gains of $20,000 per annum from the trust so that they can learn to budget, save for a house deposit and become responsible for themselves.

You then bequeath the super fund to a unit trust that keeps your family off welfare for the next two generations at least.

This is a program that will be decried by the left. But what greater gift can you give to society than to ensure that your family will never have to take from the public purse.

Conclusion

If you start from scratch and:

At 18, get a job and save $100 per week.

Get an education that allows you to get an average wage for the whole of your life.

Save up for a house like you mean it.

Learn how to run your own finances and super fund, and not pay huge fees for average performance.

Get the structure right.

Then you will have amassed $12mill (in 2018 $A.) in 100 years time and at the same time kept all your descendants off the government teat, through paying them dividends from the unit trust.

A person such as this should be held up in high regard by the government. Imagine if everybody on the average income could achieve these goals, we would be a wealthy nation.

But given the government is likely to see you as working against the nation it could be a good idea for you to find investments overseas that pay no dividends and hide your capital, as the Chinese martial artists did, until the next Ronald Reagan or Maggie Thatcher comes to Australia.

Conclusion

If you have made it this far, it is time to put all the information together.

Democracy is leading to socialism all over the world. People see the government as their future; they no longer wish to take responsibility for themselves. As a result, more and more people are reliant on the government for goods, services and income. Recent figures show only 20% of Australians pay net income tax. Therefore, it is to the financial benefit of 80% to continue down the socialist path.

Political decline has led to debt-laden economies all over the world. In Australia, not only do we have substantial government debt, but more importantly we have huge household debt. The average family is no longer paying off its mortgage; instead it is going further and further into debt. Families are re-mortgaging to fund children's education, and in many cases parents are using credit cards to fund education. Effectively, the norm is to borrow money so the family can dine out, take overseas holidays, buy new cars and renovate the house. More and more parents are turning 60 and finding they must work another 15 years just to pay off the debt. In fact, what is happening is that 90% of them are ending up on a government pension.

As a nation, we have left behind the values of free speech, free markets and taking responsibility for oneself, to satisfy the needs of minority groups. Populism and identity politics have taken over from pragmatism and realism. Today, you can buy a $16,000 battery for $3,500, with the other $12,500 being subsidised. That battery will save you $500 in electricity costs in the first year. As the battery ages, the return will drop. But the real return to the economy is 3% for the first year, diminishing every year after that.

It is beyond belief that any reasonably educated person could even contemplate this sort of behaviour as being rational, yet it is now lauded as a great initiative. Linguistic constructivism has taken the place of rational and logical debate.

For 200 years, Australia has integrated diverse cultures into a multic-ethnic community, but today we have regulated out the ability for many recent arrivals to work and therefore have assured that many immigrants are segregated by language from the wider community, resulting in suspicion and fear.

The average 20-year-old today should earn more from unearned income than from earned income in their life. You will have seen that by planning, budgeting and living within your means, it is possible to break the present cycle of entitlement and dependency and generate enough unearned income to live the life you have set for yourself. In fact, it is not all that difficult, it just requires balance.

Epilogue

The answer to a balanced life is: you find yourself the perfect life partner, then you get a dream and formulate a plan to achieve it. I met the right person right after a low point. For the first five years she was a friend, confidante and nurturer. For the next ten years, she cleaned up the messes I made, and for the next twenty years she was a partner, muse and companion.

We talked about the need to have a dreamer, an administrator and a technician in any business. The same applies in a partnership. Only the extraordinary can do it alone; therefore, the most important decision of your life is who your life partner will be.

A Schedule to
The Parallel Universe

1 The New Game 13
How to Play the game 15
The Rules 15
Your Environment 16
Skills 16
Become aware of yourself 16
Equipment 16
The Plan 17
Reframing your values and philosophies 17

2 Your Environment 19
Physical 19
Government 20
    The present 21
    Politics 23
        Equality 23
        Globalism 23
        Identity Politics 24
    Australian Government 24
        Debate 25
        Facts 25
        Language 26
            Equality 27
    Where is Politics going? 28
    The skills required for governing 30
        The Visionary 30
        The Administrator 31
        The Technician 31

Jobs of Government 31
    Policy 31
    Actions 31
    Affairs of State 31
Interaction of governing and law 32
Governance versus Politics 33
Political Debate 35
Taxation 35
    How much 36
    Collection 36
    Government need 36
    How efficient is the system? 37
    Singapore 38

The Economy 38
    The State of the Economy 40
        Companies 42
        Corporate culture 43
        Summary 44
    The Economic Debate 45
    The point 46

Culture 47
    Psychology 48
        Thought patterns and positive mental attitude 49
        Natural Methods 50
        Unnatural methods 52
    Language 52
        Technology 52
        Fashion 52
        Cultural Wars 52
        Summary 54
    Communication 55
    Negotiation 57
    Regulation 58

Social Behaviour 61
Social Behaviour as part of our DNA 63
Research 65
Customs 66
Groupthink 67
The legal system and culture 68

The Financial System 70
Financial System Basics 71
You in the System 71
Financial Service Providers 72
Financial Markets 74
Debt 74
Equity 75
Foreign Exchange 75
Derivative Markets 75
Providers of Financial Advice 75
The Regulators 76

Australia, where are you? 77
Government 77
Economy 80
Australia's national Debt Position 81
Energy 82
Rent-seeking 83
The Mindset of Australians 84
Self-reliance has moved to entitlement 84
Emphasis has moved from responsibilities to rights 85
Saving for a rainy day has moved to spend it now there will be plenty later 87
Parenting has moved from strict to lenient, from mentor to friend 88
All four of these stories are told in one story 89

　　　　The Integration of immigrants 91
　　　　Summary 91
　　Australia where will you be in 2065? 92
　　　　　Changes in the last 50 years 94
　　　　　Employment 94
　　　　　Income 95
　　　　　Governance 95
　　　　　Culture 96
　　Vision for the Future 96
　　Conclusion to Defining your Environment 97
　　　　We have learned 97
　　　　　Why do I have to do this, my parents never did? 99

3 Balance 101
　　Kudos 101
　　Lifestyle 102
　　Job Satisfaction 102
　　Financial reward 103
　　Morality/Ethics 103
　　Ethics and Morals 103
　　Social Psychopaths 104
　　When you get the balance wrong 104

4 Fifty Two Things I have Learned 105
　　1 Teamwork 105
　　2 Vision 105
　　3 Measurement 106
　　4 Authority 106
　　5 Learn to embrace hunger 107

6 H=R/E Happiness equals reality divided by expectations 108
7 The information world has swamped the thinking world 108
8 There are two things to which people completely close down: Retirement and aged care 108
9 We have become risk adverse 109
10 The 80-20 principle, Teams 109
11 The 2,2,1/2 rule is now the 4,4,1/4 rule 110
12 Gold nuggets take patience to find 110
13 10% of the population are classified as social psychopaths 111
14 Real power is hidden 111
15 The tortoise and the hare 112
16 Our moral structure has moved from church to courtroom 113
17 The four seasons 113
18 Solutions to problems and good feelings 114
19 Perceptions are real 114
20 Money does weird things to people 114
21 Failure is not only building, it is good 115
22 Balance 115
23 Lifestyle varies from the old hippies to those totally obsessed with the fast lane 116
24 Career satisfaction is something needed and in fact demanded by many 116
25 Finance 116

26 Kudos is sometimes the most difficult parameter to understand 117
27 Morals/Ethics 118
28 The growth curve 119
29 Survival attained, the drive to achieve disappears 119
30 You always need a plan B 120
31 You can't make a silk purse out of a sow's ear 120
32 Work towards getting paid for what you can do, not what you do 121
33 Problem solving 121
34 When delegating, make sure the responsibility lies with one person 122
35 Government and 1st tier business capital projects are costing three times what they need to 122
36 The 6 P's. Proper Planning Prevents Piss Poor Performance 123
37 Ways of thinking 124
38 A leader that has no followers is just someone taking a walk 125
39 Do the hardest things first 125
40 Eat breakfast like a king, lunch like a prince and dinner like a pauper 126
41 The gut buster 126
42 Routine 126
43 One of the most important lessons in life 127
44 What goes around comes around 128
45 The pendulum does swing 128
46 Do today's work today 128

47 There is no recovery 129
48 You can teach an old dog new tricks 130
49 You cannot regulate or legislate bad behaviour 130
50 Values are at the heart of our lives 131
51 True happiness always comes from outside your comfort zone 131
52 Everybody wants to be useful 131

5 Finance 133

Money 133
Precious metals 133
Coins 134
Bills of Exchange 134
Banknotes 134
Cryptocurrencies 134
Conclusion 135

The Value of Money 135

Storing Money 136
Under the bed 136
In the bank 136
Other investments 136

Saving Money 137
Income as a function of saving 137
Vehicle 137
Budgeting 138

Counting money: accounting 138
Profit and Loss (P&L) 139

Income 140
Expenses 142
Cash Flow 143
Balance Sheet 143
Taxation 144

6 Business Basics 147

Financial Goals 147

Business Roles 148
- Owner shareholder 148
- Director 148
- Manager 149
- Employee 149

Financial Roles 150
- Discretionary trust roles 151
- Self-Managed Super Fund Role 152

Funding 152

Business planning 153

Rate of Return 153

Strategy 153

Structure 153

Summary 154

7 Investment Basics 155

Introduction 155
- The 10 step problem solving process 155
- Your problems 156

Direct Investments 158
    Cash 158
        Notes and Coin 158
    Fixed interest 158
        Term deposit 158
        Bonds 158
        Hybrids 158
    Property as real property 159
        Residential 159
        Commercial 163
        Cost associated with property investments 164
        Conclusion 165
    REIT's: Real Estate Investment Trusts 165
    Equities 165
        Shares 166
        Valuation of equities 166
        Rights issues 168
        Share Purchase Plans 168
        Cost associated with Equity Transactions 168
        Hedge Funds 169
        EFT's: Exchange Traded Funds 170
        Listed investment companies (LIC's) 171
    Equities versus Real Estate 173
    Derivatives 175
    Infrastructure 175
    Transparency 176

Managed investments 176
    Investment Management 177
        Theories of investment management 178
            Active management 178
            Hedge funds 178
            Passive management 179
            Absolute return 179
            Conviction management 179

Value Adding 180
Diversification 180

Portfolio Management 181
Borrowing Basics: Loans 182
Home Loans 183
Investment Loans 183
Types of investment Loans 183
Principle and Interest 183
Interest only 183
Line of Credit 183
Other options 184
Margin loan 184
Reverse Mortgage 184

Investment Objectives 184
Preservation of capital 184
Current income 185
Purchase a home 185
Educate children 185
Retirement living 186
Holidays 186
Toys 186

Investment Strategies 186
Value investing 186
Growth investing 187
Technical Analysis 187
Contrarian Investing 187
Thematic Investing 188

Investment plan 188
Risk Management 188
General insurance 190

Life insurance 190
  Business overhead insurance 192
Net return 192
  Earnings 192
  Expenses 193
  Tax 193
Legal Entities 193
  Individual 193
  Sole trader 193
  Personal Services Income (PSI) 194
  Partnership 194
  Private Company 195
  Public Company 195
  Not for profit organisation 195
  Incorporated association 195
  Discretionary trust 196
  Testamentary trusts 196
  Superannuation Fund 196

Legal Structures 200
The Concept of Wealth 200
  Unearned income 201
  Lazy Money 202
  Creating wealth 202
    Generating capital 202
    Rate of return 204
    Structure 205
    Strategy 205
      Set your vision 206
      Plan to achieve the vision 206
      Pick your specialities 206
      Pick your specialists 206

Intergenerational Wealth 207
  Intergenerational wealth structure 209
  Socialist versus capitalist 210
  Hero or Zero 211
The Future 212

8 Who are you? 215
You as an individual 215
Personality 216
Values 216
Beliefs 217
Politics 218
Financial 220
Cultural 221
Opportunities 221
Threats 223
  Physical 223
  Relationship 223
Strengths 224
Weaknesses 224
Strategic Competitive Advantages 224
Conclusion 225

9 Your Vision 227
Total Vision 228
Job Satisfaction 228
Lifestyle 229

Finance 229
Kudos 229
Morals/Ethics 229

10 Your Plan 231
Career 232
Lifestyle 234
Finance 235
    The Value of Money 236
    Educating children 237
    Insurance 237
    Divorce 238
Family 239

11 A Standard Plan 241
Budget 241
The House 243
    Deposit 243
    The Mortgage 244
The Kids Education 244
Superannuation and Retirement planning 245
    Life Expectancy 246
    Retiring Age 247
    The need for retirement funding 247
        How long? 247
        How Much? 247
        Health 247
        Lifestyle 247

What are the options for retirement planning 249
The Status Quo 249
How to achieve the objective? 250

Intergenerational Wealth Creation 252
Scenario 1 251
Scenario 2 251
Scenario 3 253
Scenario 4 253

Conclusion 255

Epilogue 257

www.ingramcontent.com/pod-product-compliance
Lightning Source LLC
Chambersburg PA
CBHW071833230426
43671CB00012B/1949